THE PERSISTENT PROBLEMS OF EDUCATION

by
Paul Woodring

Distinguished Service Professor
of the University, Emeritus
Western Washington University
Bellingham, Washington

A Publication of the Phi Delta Kappa Educational Foundation
Bloomington, Indiana

Cover design by Nancy Rinehart

Library of Congress Catalogue Card Number 83-61656
ISBN 0-87367-428-6
Printed in the United States of America

To Jeannette

This monograph is sponsored by the University of Southern California Chapter of Phi Delta Kappa, which made a generous contribution toward publication costs.

Contents

Preface

All social movements involve conflicts which are reflected intellectually in controversies. It would not be a sign of health if such an important social interest as education were not also an arena of struggles, practical and theoretical.[1]

John Dewey

Debates over education are staged in many arenas: courtrooms, legislative committees, school board meetings, parent-teacher interchanges, curriculum committee meetings, newspapers, magazines, and books, as well as over the family dinner table. Over the years some problems are solved, some controversies subside. The debate over coeducation in public schools came to an end a long time ago. The controversy over the legitimacy of using public funds for the support of secondary schools was resolved a century ago by various state supreme courts, most notably in the *Kalamazoo* case of 1874. The decision to eliminate racial segregation, though not yet fully implemented, was firmly made in 1954 by the U.S. Supreme Court.

But other controversies continue for years, decades, or centuries. While some of these, as Dewey pointed out, are both practical and theoretical, the underlying theoretical issues are often unclear to participants in the debate. The controversy over the teaching of evolution, for example, rests on different answers to the question, "In our quest for knowledge and understanding shall

1

we rely on faith and revealed truth or on empirical evidence and rational thought?'' Until agreement is reached on that — and no such agreement is in sight — the debate will continue.

Controversy continues to rage over the meaning, purpose, and goals of education, the cost of schools, the content of the curriculum, school prayer, sex education, methods of teaching, textbooks, discipline, the competence of teachers, and a host of other problems.

These persistent problems are ones with two or more sides that can be defended by informed people with strong convictions. The failure to solve them does not result from lack of research. Investigators have received massive grants from foundations and the federal government; their findings clog the shelves of university libraries. And yet the problems persist. Some of them seem no closer to solution than they were two or three generations ago. Why?

This monograph is an attempt to answer that question. I am not so optimistic as to think that another book will solve problems of such complexity. The best I can hope is that I may be able to define the issues, explore the underlying reasons for disagreement, illuminate the dark corners, offer some historical perspective, and perhaps help teachers to think more calmly and reasonably about the problems while the search for answers continues.

The American educational enterprise is so vast, complex, and confusing that no individual has a clear picture of it all. Even if he has read widely of the literature, has some familiarity with the statistics, and has visited schools all across the land, his views inevitably are colored by his more limited personal experience as student and teacher. Consequently it seems only fair that when he writes a book about education he should let his readers know something about the personal background that provides the basis for his conclusions, convictions, and biases.

I have lived long enough to have observed many of the changes that have occurred during the twentieth century, and length of view gives perspective even though it gives no assurance of wisdom. I entered the first grade in a rural consolidated school in northwestern Ohio in 1913 and later attended a one-room country school for three years. I entered Delta High School in 1921 when it had an enrollment of less than 200. I entered Bowling Green State Normal (which despite its name was already a four-year, degree-granting college) in 1925. After two years of college, I began teaching in a country elementary school in 1927, first taught in a suburban high school in 1930 (after taking my bachelor's degree at Bowling Green), took my Ph.D. at Ohio State in 1938, and began my career of teaching future teachers at what was then Western Washington College of Education in 1939.

I did not begin writing about the problems of education until 1952 when I was already 45 and a tenured full professor. Consequently, none of my writing about education has been motivated by a desire for academic promotion or career advancement. I wrote because there were things I wanted to say and felt needed saying to a large audience, which includes people who are not educators but are deeply concerned about school problems.

My years as consultant to the Fund for the Advancement of Education and educational advisor to the Ford Foundation gave me an opportunity to visit many schools and colleges of education and to talk with educators. During my 10 years as education editor, and later editor-at-large, for *Saturday Review* I learned a great deal about the problems of education by reading hundreds of manuscripts (many of which we had no room to print) plus thousands of letters to the editor from teachers, students, and parents. I am grateful to all these for the contribution they made to my education.

I am grateful also to the thousands of students who have been in my classes over the past 55 years and have contributed as much to my education as I have to theirs. Although the major part of my college teaching has been at Western Washington University, I have had the opportunity, as a visiting professor, to work with future teachers at Carleton College, San Jose State, and the University of California at Berkeley.

In preparing this manuscript I have borrowed occasional paragraphs from my earlier works — speeches, articles, editorials, and books. But, as William James said when he found himself doing the same thing while writing his *Talks to Teachers*, "I have even copied several pages verbatim, but I do not know that apology is needed for plagiarism such as this."[2]

---

1. John Dewey, *Experience and Education* (New York: Macmillan Inc., 1939), p. v.
2. William James, *Talks to Teachers*, Norton Edition (New York: W. W. Norton & Co., 1958), p. 19.

1

What Education
Is of Most Worth?

*All men do not agree on what they would have a child learn. From
the present mode of education we cannot determine with certainty to
which men incline; whether to instruct a child in what will be useful to
him in life, or what tends to virtue, or that is excellent, for all these
things have their separate defenders.*[1]

Aristotle

The disagreement observed by Aristotle was old in his time, has persisted
through the centuries, and plagues us today. Wherever an authoritarian
church or ruler is in control, it may be suppressed; but wherever citizens are
free to express their opinions, it comes to the forefront of controversy. It is the
source of debates over the relative merits of vocational and liberal education;
it fuels the demand for basic education; it underlies controversies over the
need for physical education, sex education, driver training, moral instruction,
and recreational activities in the schools. It is a problem for which there are no
final answers, but it is one that cannot be ignored because no schooling can be
planned and no curriculum can be constructed without at least a tentatively
agreed-upon answer.

Today, as in Aristotle's time, each kind of education has its separate

4

defenders, who state a preference and then contend that their favorite subject or goal is being neglected and deserves a larger portion of the school's time and resources. Often the defenders are teachers of the subject, and they can make a persuasive case for more of their specialty, because it is true that nothing is given as much time or taught as well as could be wished.

When parents are asked why they want their sons and daughters to get a good education they are likely to say, "Because we want them to have a better life than we have had," or "Because we want them to get ahead in the world." By "getting ahead" they probably mean finding a better paid, more pleasant, and more secure job. Thus students are likely to select a course of study in terms of job preparation and, whenever possible, to avoid subjects unrelated to that goal.

In sharp contrast, most educational philosophers, as well as other well-educated men and women who have thought long and deeply about it, reject the view that preparation for work is the primary goal of education. The proper goals, they contend, are the pursuit of wisdom, the development of human potential, and the search for understanding the nature of human beings and their world. However their goals are stated, they insist that preparing a student for a specific vocation is only a secondary goal and that the desire to make more money is not properly an educational goal.

Even parents who think first of vocational preparation see a need for the many goals of education and find it difficult to choose among them. When asked by Gallup pollsters, "What should get *more* attention in the schools?" 80% to 90% say "Career education." But in response to another question, 83% say there is need for *more* basic education. And 85% say that extracurricular activities such as sports, dramatics, bands, and school newspapers are "very important" or "fairly important."[2]

Students are equally confused. When high school seniors were queried by the National Center for Education Statistics in 1980, 71.7% said the schools they had attended should have placed more emphasis on "academics" and then, reversing themselves, 75.2% said that more should have been placed on vocational preparation.[3]

This is the dilemma: Since student time as well as school resources are limited, more attention to one subject or goal means less attention to something else. At one time educators hoped that by lengthening the school year and keeping children in school for more years it would be possible to achieve all the desired goals. It has not become possible and there is little likelihood that any further extension of time will solve the problem. Who, then, should determine the priorities, and on what basis?

In a self-governing nation the public schools must be responsive to the public will, but the poll results make it apparent that the public will cannot be determined by asking people to vote on separate issues without time for thought. Those who make educational decisions must ask themselves what

5

priorities the people would choose if they were well-informed, thought clearly, acted rationally, and took a long-range view of the goals of education.

Liberal Education in the Public Schools

We call those studies liberal that are worthy of free men.

Seneca

Today we are committed to the view that all men and women must be free; it follows that all must be liberally educated. Not all will go to college, however, and if these students do not get a liberal education in the elementary and secondary schools, they will not get it anywhere. And they will need it.

The goal of liberal education is to free individuals from the limitations of ignorance, prejudice, and provincialism; to enable them to see the world clearly and in perspective; to develop their intellectual capacities, increase their sensitivity, and prepare them to make wise, independent judgments. When speaking of such goals for the public schools, many educators prefer the term *general education*. But this term is too vague. It lacks a sense of purpose and has no tradition behind it. It is too easily interpreted to mean a random selection of courses without integration and with no clear goals. Academic scholars and other intellectuals who are critical of the public schools assume that because educators avoid the word *liberal* they do not endorse the concept. We can go a long way toward closing the breach between secondary and higher education by using the traditional term that has the support of the community of scholars.

Throughout the world a major part of the responsibility for liberal education has always been accepted by intermediate and secondary schools. The great German universities of the nineteenth century had no liberal arts colleges; students were expected to get their liberal education in a secondary school — the *real gymnasium* — before entering the university. In England the clusters of small residential colleges that constituted the universities at Oxford and Cambridge had more liberal aims, but they admitted younger students, including many of high school age. And the education provided by English lower schools was also liberal. Shakespeare, with only the education provided by a sixteenth century "grammar school," was well acquainted with the history of many nations and with the literature of Greece and Rome.

The high school senior reading *Hamlet*, the sophomore studying geometry, the seventh-grader encountering for the first time the principles of evolution, even the fifth-grader reading *Treasure Island*, are getting a liberal education. They are not merely preparing themselves to get a liberal education *after* they enter college. The failure of college professors to understand this is seen in the custom of referring to secondary institutions as "prep schools." But a high school, whether public or private, is no more a prep school than is a college; it

6

is education itself. Liberal education begins as soon as a child has learned to read. By denying the responsibility of public school teachers for liberal education, we have demeaned their role.

Liberal education should not be confused with the *liberal arts* as they are taught in college. Liberal education is a goal; liberal arts is a curriculum designed to be one way of reaching that goal. While the goal has remained relatively constant over the centuries, the curriculum designed to achieve it has changed dramatically and continues to change.

The concept of liberal education came to us from Greece, where the liberal arts considered appropriate to the free man of Athens included grammar, gymnastics, music, and sometimes drawing at the elementary level, and logic, rhetoric, philosophy, arithmetic, geometry, astronomy and musical harmony at the higher level. The Romans added to the list. But in the fourth century A.D., Martianus Capella reduced the curriculum to seven subjects, which later became the basis for medieval education. These consisted of a trivium: grammar, rhetoric, and logic; and a quadrivium: arithmetic, geometry, astronomy, and music.

Each of these seven had a wider meaning than it has today. Grammar often included a study of literature; rhetoric included the development of skills in written as well as oral expression; and logic included much of philosophy. Music, in Greece, included poetry and dancing; arithmetic included a study of the mystical significance and properties of numbers.

It was the Roman scholars of the first century A.D. who first emphasized the importance of the classics in liberal education. To the Latin scholar "classical" meant having its origin in Greece. Since the days of Rome the idea that a liberal education must have deep roots in the past has become well established; but it is worthy of mention that the Greeks themselves placed little emphasis on the importance of antiquity (except for the narrative poetry of Homer) and did not consider a study of foreign languages essential to the educated man. "The Greeks," said Sainte-Beuve, "had no classics but themselves."

Of the seven liberal arts of the medieval schools, at least two, grammar and arithmetic, are now taught in elementary schools. Geometry is taught in high school and music at all levels. Rhetoric is rarely taught as a separate course (although anyone who listens to the speeches of today's politicians can see a need for it), and logic rarely is taught as a separate course below the college level. Elements of astronomy may be found in junior high general science courses, but astronomy as a separate course is no longer required at any level.

During the Middle Ages it was essential for a scholar to know Latin or Greek or both if he were to have anything important to read, because the vernacular languages had not yet developed literature of much importance. Until at least the middle of the nineteenth century, American liberal arts colleges and the secondary schools that prepared students for them spent a large part of their time teaching the languages and literature of Greece and Rome. The value of these languages as a part of liberal education is still debated, but the absolute need for them as an open door to the world of books has steadily declined with the development of English and American literature and modern science, plus adequate translations of most of the classical literature. The decline of emphasis on the classics made room for many other subjects.

Today it is generally agreed that the liberal curriculum must include the physical, biological, and social sciences as well as mathematics, philosophy, languages and literatures, art, and music. Many, if not all, of these obviously belong in the public school curriculum and can be as liberal there as they are when taught in college.

But course titles and subject matter content alone do not make a program liberal. More important is the way it is taught and the way it is used. George Stoddard, speaking in 1962 to the American Association of Land Grant Colleges and State Universities, proposed four tests that should be applied in deciding whether an academic program can properly be called liberal:

1. The subject matter is enduring. It must not be ephemeral, trivial, or simply descriptive. There is a search for abstract principles, generatives, and art forms — for all that gives meaning and value to life. How-to-do-it courses cannot meet this test.
2. The subject matter is whole. It cannot be simply a segment with no beginning and no end. However brief the course, it will start with questions and bring to bear on these questions the wisdom of the ages and of contemporary thinkers. The course may end with more questions, and perhaps few answers, but it will require the student to think for himself.
3. The student, at the time, approaches the subject matter without reference to technical applications. He may like it just as much, for all that, and will work hard on it. It will not take him long to discover that he is achieving a new literacy that will brighten his life on many occasions and in all cultures. He will discern, faintly at first, and then with appreciation, an interchange between what he learns in the periphery and what he most needs at the heart-center of a specialized career.
4. Liberal education provides a common language. In liberal education we acquire a language that all persons may employ apart from "shop talk." Technical fields should contribute richly to the pool of communicable knowledge. Every informed person has an interest in mathematics, physics, chemistry, geology, astronomy, biology, anthropology, psychology, and sociology, but there must be some principle of selection for the nonspecialist. An advanced subject is not of itself liberal. As we move up in physics, biology, economics, or logic, the subject matter actually becomes less liberal — less communicable to others. There may be less communication even among members of the field. In other words, liberal education, while based upon the most advanced thinking and creating, is a form of intellectual currency that can be acquired to some degree by every student.[4]

A liberal education, so defined, can be made available in a variety of ways. It can be organized around the traditional academic disciplines or reorganized into larger patterns that cut across the boundaries of the disciplines. It can focus on historical periods, cultures, or geographic regions. It can be taught by means of a selection of great books or great ideas. The curriculum is less important than the attitudes of teachers and students and the methods of inquiry employed. If teachers are wise and well informed, they can make a substantial contribution to students' liberal education in any course.

These liberal goals are threatened in today's universities by the demands of faculty members for ever-greater and earlier specialization, plus the demands of graduate professional schools that the undergraduate college become a prep school for the professional schools. Today's professors in all the arts and sciences show more interest in narrow specialization, and in the depth of knowledge that such specialization makes possible, than in the broader kind of liberal education that, they contend, is shallow and superficial. As a result, recent college graduates have probably spent only a small proportion of their undergraduate years in pursuit of the liberal goals and a much larger part in pursuit of the specialized studies that will get them into graduate or professional school.

This trend has been clear for at least the past 30 years. Jacques Barzun, long a champion of liberal education, found that, when he became provost at Columbia University, he could do little to stem the drift. He lamented, "The liberal arts tradition is dead or dying . . . the trend seems to me so clear that to object would be like trying to sweep back the ocean." He meant, of course, that the tradition is dying in colleges and universities. If this is true, and I fear it is, there is all the greater need for pursuit of the liberal goals of education at the secondary level where it still has a chance to survive.

Vocational Goals

The European practice of sorting out children at an early age and providing liberal education only for those who are bound for the universities, while shunting others directly into trade schools, is contrary to the American tradition and inappropriate in a nation that can afford to provide 12 years of schooling for all plus higher education for many. We do not accept the view that the kind and quality of secondary education should depend on social class. Nevertheless, most of our high schools offer a variety of programs from which students may choose. One sequence of courses is designed specifically for those who wish to prepare for college, a second, and often less demanding program, is offered those who do not plan to go to college, and still a third program is available for those who want vocational preparation in high school.

Because unskilled jobs are becoming rare, it is obvious that youth must, at some time and in some way, be trained or educated for their life's work. Though it is not quite so obvious, it is generally agreed by parents, school board members, legislators, and employers that some part of the preparation — for those who are not going on to higher institutions of learning — is a responsibility of the public schools. Yet the debate over vocational education in high school has been long and acrimonious.

The questions that divide us and are legitimate subject for debate are these:

1. How much basic, general, or liberal education should precede vocational education and how much should be concurrent with it?

2. What portion of the student's time and of the school's resources should be devoted to vocational education at each level of schooling?

3. At what age should vocational education begin? If the answer is that it depends on the individual, what are the proper criteria for distinguishing among individuals?

4. Should vocational education be preparation for entry into specific jobs as they exist today or for lifetime careers in broad vocational areas in which the skills required for specific jobs may change rapidly? (If it is to be education in the broader sense, is it really vocational or general?)

5. What are the responsibilities of other agencies and institutions? What kinds of vocational training are best provided through an apprenticeship program or on-the-job training rather than in schools?

The persistence of the debate reflects the fact that those who make the decisions have failed to ask themselves these questions. Congress passed the Smith-Hughes Act providing for vocational education in 1917 — long before it provided any financial support for basic, general, or liberal education.

Most children at age 14 do not know what vocations they will pursue. While some broad exploratory courses in vocations can be justified, the more specific kinds of vocational preparation are not appropriate until the student has made a firm vocational choice. Many who undertake extended periods of vocational preparation in high school later pursue vocations unrelated to training. Gordon Swanson, past president of the American Vocational Association, writing in *Phi Delta Kappan* (October 1978, p. 89) quotes from a report of the American Institutes for Research that says, "About 65% of the vocational graduates enter the trade for which trained or one related to it." Whether this indicates a total waste of time and effort for the other 35% depends on whether the training was narrowly specialized or sufficiently broad to have some liberal value, but the figure clearly suggests that the selective process leaves much to be desired.

Vocational *training* and vocational *education* are not synonyms even though careless writers often use them interchangeably. *Training* is the appropriate word for teaching specific skills that require little or no background knowledge and can be taught in a single course with no prerequisites. Vocational *education* is a more appropriate term for a sequence of courses that prepares a student for a variety of related activities such as those required in farming or homemaking. Students enrolled in a course in agriculture probably have learned from their parents how a farm is operated today; what they need to gain in school is an understanding of plant and animal biology, soil chemistry, and business management in preparation for the changes that will come in farming during their lifetimes. Future homemakers (male and female) need a knowledge of human biology, the chemistry of foods, child psychology, budgeting, and family planning, much of which will be gained in courses not specifically labeled *vocational*. Carpenters must learn that the length of a rafter is the hypotenuse of a right-angled triangle, that a room or house can be made rectangular by the application of principles of plane geometry. They need an understanding of the strength of materials, including the various kinds of lumber, as well as the nature and uses of many kinds of tools. An electrician needs a knowledge of electricity. Thus, because all the highly skilled trades require mathematical and scientific knowledge as well as skills, preparation for them is properly called vocational *education*.

Since the 1960s, when then U. S. Commissioner of Education Sydney Marland was strongly advocating "career education," the term has often been misused as a fancy term for vocational education. But *career* is defined by Webster as "a course of continued progress in the life of a person." Preparation for a single job or vocation cannot be called career education without doing violence to the English language. It seems apparent that typical unskilled or semiskilled laborers have no great desire for a career — what they want are safe, secure jobs with good pay and fringe benefits.

There are careers in auto manufacturing, but not on the assembly line. *Career* implies upward movement. Preparation for a career in industry, business, art, music, writing and editing, diplomacy, government, or the military may begin in the elementary and secondary schools but must be continued in institutions of higher learning. The most appropriate place for career education is a graduate or professional school or a specialized institution such as a music conservatory or an institute of technology.

Most vocational teachers will agree that the scope of vocational programs in high school should be sufficiently broad to minimize the danger that skills acquired will soon be made obsolete by technological change. It was not sound use of a school's resources to train large numbers of riveters at a time when riveters were about to be replaced by welders or to train elevator operators just a few years before elevators were to become automatic. Even though the immediate goal of many students is to start out in a well-paid job, without much thought to the long future, the goal of their teachers and of those who plan vocational programs should be preparation for a lifetime in a rapidly changing world.

Vocational preparation has never been, and should not be, the exclusive responsibility of schools. Whether work is in a factory, the building trades, an office, or a profession, employers, through their older and more experienced workers, have a responsibility for a substantial amount of on-the-job training. Unfortunately, some employers have found it profitable to let the schools do all the training so that new employees will already have been sorted out and taught all the details of their work. Some vocational educators have been eager to accept the full responsibility because it means more jobs for them. But educators who want to make the most of the time and resources available to the schools would be wise to pass some of the responsibility back to employers, limiting the school's responsibility to teaching those things that are learned more effectively and more economically in school than on the job.

People who stress the importance of vocational education point to the fact that some liberally educated graduates cannot find immediate employment; and even those who do sometimes have to accept lower beginning salaries than those who are prepared for a specific vocation. People who stress the liberal goals respond that life is more than work: individuals who leave school at 18 or 22, work a 40-hour week until retirement age, and then live to be 80, will spend no more than one-fourth of their waking hours on the job. Education should prepare them for all of life — not for just working life. They contend that vocational education does not prepare students for the decisions they must make as free citizens, for the appreciation of beauty, or for thinking deeply about the things that matter most. And they add that at best a vocational education prepares an individual only for entry into a first job — not for the changes that are sure to come during that individual's lifetime. A more general or liberal education, because it is preparation for versatility, is the best preparation for those who will live in a changing world.

Although these seem to be persuasive arguments, the liberal tradition has always had to fight for its existence because its values, which are delayed and intangible, are not readily apparent to practical people. The many citizens who prefer a kind of education that yields more immediate results exert great pressure on school boards and legislative bodies. As a result of these pressures the total expenditures of federal, state, and local governments for vocational education in the United States increased from 128 million dollars in 1950 to 6.4 *billion* dollars in 1979 and continues to rise at a rate of about one billion dollars each year.[5]

No one need fear for the future of vocational education. Employers want it, parents want it, legislators want it, and many students prefer it. The future of liberal education is far more precarious.

Progressive vs. Conservative Goals

The Progressive Education Movement, which dominated educational literature and many teachers colleges (though not nearly all the schools) from early in this century until about 1950, has passed into history. Writing in 1961, Lawrence Cremin said:

> The death of the Progressive Education Association in 1955 and the passing of its journal *Progressive Education* two years later marked the end of an era in American pedagogy. Yet one would hardly have known it from the pitifully small group of mourners at both funerals. Somehow, a movement that for a half a century, enlisted the enthusiasms, the loyalty, the imagination, and the energy of a large segment of the American public and the teaching profession became, in the decade following World War II, anathema, immortalized only in jokes.[6]

But though the movement is gone, some of its goals had become so widely accepted and so nearly achieved, that they remain embedded in American schools even though the word "Progressive" is no longer attached to them. Today's schools in smaller cities, towns, and rural areas (perhaps less so in large central cities) are happier places for children than they were in 1900. Old jokes about children hating school, fearing their teachers, and being reluctant to return to school in September have much less meaning to today's children than they did to their grandparents. Teachers now have a better understanding of children and of the nature of the learning process and are better aware of individual differences in learning capacity. More teachers now use student interests as a source of motivation.

One progressive goal, however, continues to be controversial — the effort to broaden the scope of education to include the total development of the whole child by accepting responsibilities that had once been those of other institutions or agencies.

In 1899 John Dewey, in *School and Society*, called attention to the fact that, as a result of urbanization and industrialization, many responsibilities that had traditionally been accepted by the family, the neighborhood, the church, and the workplace were no longer being accepted by any of these institutions. The school, said Dewey, must now accept them.

Educators interpreted this to mean that if the home and community were not making adequate provision for social and recreational activities, the school must provide them. If children came to school without an adequate diet, the school should supplement it. If girls were no longer receiving instruction in homemaking from their mothers, the schools should offer instruction in what was then called "domestic science." If boys were not learning a trade from their fathers or through the apprenticeship system, the school must offer vocational training. And if children were not adequately counseled at home, the school should do the counseling.

This view of the school as a *legatee* institution had, by the 1930s, become one of the cornerstones of the Progressive movement and one accepted by many schools. It greatly expanded the scope of education; it also added to the cost. The broader emphasis undoubtedly enriched the lives of children from inadequate homes but led to complaints from more responsible parents that the schools were taking over responsibilities that were not properly education, that did not belong in the school, and that parents would prefer to accept themselves. As a result, there was increasing criticism that the more basic functions of school were being neglected. "Time was," said one unhappy father, "when I took my children to the circus and teachers taught them to read. Now the teachers take them to the circus and I must teach them to read."

One long-term result of such parental discontent was the back-to-basics movement that gained prominence some four decades later. A more immediate result was that a great many Americans, laymen as well as educators, set out to redefine the goals of education and the school's responsibility. But some of the first efforts only added to the confusion because these groups produced long lists of goals with no indication of priorities.

Someone has said that the reason for the brevity of the Ten Commandments is that they were not written by a committee. Unfortunately, many of the statements of education goals are the work of large groups, the members of which find it necessary to compromise their positions before agreement can be reached.

In 1938 the Educational Policies Commission, a distinguished body of men and women who were then among the leaders of American education, drew up a list of 43 educational goals including such things as the inquiring mind, reading, sight and hearing, recreation, friendship, courtesy, cooperation, homemaking, public health, efficiency in buying, consumer protection, world citizenship, economic literacy, and a desire to be a "participant and spectator in many sports and other pastimes." There was something here for everyone, whether the school was viewed as a custodial institution, a playground, a hospital, a propaganda agency, or an educational institution.

Many educators accepted this long list of goals because it seemed consistent with Dewey's view of the school as a *legatee* institution. But it was of little use to curriculum makers and other educational planners because it seemed to justify as an educational objective everything that even the most visionary person could suggest as an experience or activity appropriate to the good life. It gave approval to a continued expansion of the school's role and further proliferation of both curricular and extracurricular activities. It opened the door to all kinds of pressure on the schools to accept ever-increasing responsibilities.

After World War II laymen developed greater interest in educational problems and joined with educators in their efforts to clarify objectives. The White House Conference on Education in 1955 included 1,800 delegates from all parts of the nation. Their conference report offered the following statement of the schools' responsibilities:

It is the consensus of these groups that the schools should continue to develop:

1. The fundamental skills of communication — reading, writing, spelling, as well as other elements of effective oral and written expression; the arithmetical and mathematical skills including problem solving.
2. Appreciation of our democratic heritage.
3. Civic rights and responsibilities and knowledge of American institutions.
4. Respect and appreciation for human values and for the beliefs of others.
5. Ability to think and evaluate constructively and creatively.
6. Effective work habits and self-discipline.
7. Social competency as contributing members of the family and community.
8. Ethical behavior based on a sense of moral and spiritual values.

9. Intellectual curiosity and eagerness for lifelong learning.
10. Aesthetic appreciation and self-expression in the arts.
11. Physical and mental health.
12. Wise use of time, including constructive leisure pursuits.
13. Understanding of the physical world and man's relation to it as represented through basic knowledge of the sciences.
14. Awareness of our relationship with the world community.

It is significant to note the changes in emphasis that occurred between 1938 and 1955. The White House Conference list (which is much shorter than the one of 1938) omits such goals as "efficiency in buying," "consumer protection," and "courtesy," which were stressed in 1938. And we were no longer told that every educated person must be a participant in "many sports and pastimes."

But the White House Conference Report still has limitations. It fails to discriminate between obvious educational goals, such as the ability to think and to communicate through the written word, and other goals, such as health, for which another profession bears the major responsibility. And although the report stressed the need for priorities, "We recommend that school authorities emphasize the importance of priorities in education — It is essential that schools pursue a policy of giving children first things first," it did not indicate what these priorities should be.

At about mid-century another group of educators took the position that the major goal should be children's adjustment to their physical and social environment. But "Life Adjustment Education," as it was called, came under sharp attack from those who said that social adjustment is too easily confused with conformity and that adjustment to the world of today may be poor preparation for the world of tomorrow. They added that people should be prepared to change and improve the world rather than adapt themselves to the world as it is. Although Life Adjustment Education was a favorite target of critics in the 1950s, it had a small following and a short life. It was never a significant aspect of Progressive education and was never a dominant philosophy in many American schools.

The conservative view of education stands in sharp contrast to the progressive view. During the Thirties, Forties, and Fifties a few distinguished professors of education — William Bagley and later Isaac Kandel, Ross Finney, H. H. Horn, J. Donald Butler, and Robert Ulich — continued to stress the importance of traditional goals. Philosophically, some of these were idealists while others were realists, but they shared the conviction that there are certain stable truths and values that children should learn.

A larger number of spokesmen for the conservative position were university presidents or professors in arts and sciences, who had a scholarly knowledge of their disciplines but a more limited understanding of the problems of educating children, some of whom inevitably are of modest academic talent.

Progressives often accused such conservative educators of placing an exaggerated emphasis on learning facts, but this was not an accurate interpretation of their intent. The purpose of education, said Robert Maynard Hutchins, " is not to teach men facts, theories, or laws . . . it is to unsettle their minds, widen their horizons, inflame their intellects, teach them to think straight if possible, but to think always for themselves."[7]

Arthur Bestor, a vigorous and sometimes strident critic of progressive education and of professional educators, said, "The learning of facts is not intellectual training unless those facts are seen as the conclusion of systematic inquiry, and as part of a larger structure of knowledge," and "The liberal disciplines are not chunks of frozen fact. They are not facts at all. They are the powerful tools and engines by which a man discovers and handles facts. Without the scientific and scholarly disciplines he is helpless in the presence of 'facts'."[8]

"The liberal studies," said President Whitney Griswold of Yale, "are not a body of revealed truths or logical absolutes or a quantum of knowledge. They are studies designed to develop to capacity the intellectual and spiritual powers of the individual. Their aim is to make the most of man in order that he may make the most of his calling, his cultural opportunities, and his responsibilities as a citizen."[9]

These three men were regarded by professional educators as archconservatives, yet it is clear from their own statements that none of them saw the learning of facts as the aim or purpose of education. They, like many historians and classicists who take the long-range view, believed that a proper goal of education is to assure cultural continuity; and that a knowledge of the literature, philosophy, art, science, and history of the past is the best preparation for the future because it enables children to participate fully in their culture.

National Goals

After the launching of Sputnik in 1957, Admiral Hyman Rickover became the spokesman for a group of Americans who believed we should shift our emphasis from personal to national goals. Alarmed by the threat of nuclear annihilation, they saw national survival as a goal — perhaps *the* goal — of education and said that unless we survive as a free nation other goals are futile. They held that only an education specifically designed to nourish scientific and technological talent could save us. This concern was reflected in the National Defense Act of 1958, which provided for nurturing talent and improving instruction in mathematics, science, and foreign languages but gave no assistance to other liberal and humanistic disciplines.

Although the new emphasis on quality was welcome, many educators became fearful of the neglect of those disciplines not closely related to manpower needs. Clarence Faust, then president of the Fund for the Advancement of Education, said:

There are already signs that many parents are disinclined to bring up their children as manpower resources. . . . Preoccupation with the manpower aspects of education, however statesmanlike, runs into the fundamental question of whether the individual exists for society or society for the individual. On this question, the American commitment would seem to be clear, that the individual is not primarily to be regarded as a resource of the state but the state as a means for assuring the full flowering of the individual. [10]

This disagreement emphasizes a fundamental difference between self-governing nations and totalitarian nations. Nationalistic leaders such as Hitler, Stalin, and Mao have always regarded the schools as instruments of the state. In their nations, teachers and curricula were selected to foster the interests of the state. The inevitable result of such goals is conflict between nations — perpetual warfare. But preparation for living on a small planet that is fast becoming a global village cannot safely be restricted to learning the values of one nation, one political philosophy, one religion, or one culture. Norman Cousins puts it well:

The great failure of education — not just in the U.S. but throughout the world — is that it has made people become tribe-conscious rather than species-conscious. It has put limited identification ahead of ultimate identification. It has attached value to things man does but not to what man is. Man's institutions are celebrated but not man himself. Man's power is heralded but the preciousness of life is unsung. There are national anthems, but no anthems for humanity. [11]

Finding the Proper Balance

The history of education has been one long struggle between those who would educate for immediate practical ends and those who take a longer view. The curricula in most of today's schools represent an uneasy compromise between these two views — a compromise made necessary by the fact that most parents as well as most educators are unwilling to deny the importance of either goal. Is there a possibility of achieving both goals with the same program? Perhaps there is.

The various categories of education — basic, general, liberal, specialized, vocational, and professional — are so inextricably interrelated that it is impossible to distinguish clearly among them. First-grade teachers helping children learn to read are engaged in basic education while, at the same time, preparing the children for future education, both vocational and liberal, as well as for a good life in a literate society. Science teachers may view their job as a part of liberal education or as preparation for later specialization in any of many vocations. If they see the potential vocational applications of their subject, they can contribute to those applications and, at the same time, make the course more interesting without departing from their basic goals. Professors of educational philosophy or child psychology, if they do their work well, contribute as much to the liberal as to the professional education of their students.

Professional education may properly be called vocational but, because it rests upon substantial bodies of scholarly knowledge, a university can prepare students for the learned professions without departing from its traditional academic and scholarly emphasis. A course in Greek tragedy is liberal for most people but has vocational implications for future authors and for teachers of literature. A course in law may be narrowly professional, but if it deals with the history and philosophy of justice, it can be liberal.

When a high school undertakes to prepare students for vocational skills such as welding, bookkeeping, beauty culture, or barbering it introduces subject matter foreign to the traditions of scholarly education, but a well-taught course in vocational agriculture can contribute notably to the student's understanding of botany, zoology, and chemistry and hence has liberal value.

Much depends on the teachers, their wisdom, breadth of understanding, and the goals they set for themselves and their students. A first course in Latin should be liberal, but the one I took in high school was nothing more than a laborious exercise in conjugating verbs and declining nouns. It had no liberal value whatever because the teacher had no understanding of such values. But if vocational teachers understand the value and goals of liberal education, they can contribute notably to their students' achievement. If they are scornful of such goals, they will contribute nothing to their students and will cause students to share their scorn.

One reason for the continuing debate is that teachers, early in their careers, select a specialty consistent with their interests and talents; having made this choice, they soon become convinced that the subject or specialty to which they have decided to devote their career is receiving less than its share of time and support. When they become a member of a curriculum committee or chairman of a department, they fight for their own subject or specialty without giving sufficient thought to the total education of the student.

What is most needed is educational planners who take a longer view, who have an understanding of the uses of all possible subjects of instruction, who are aware of the long process of development that provides the basis for our present culture and society, who are fully aware that pupils now in school will spend their adult lives in the twenty-first century, and who understand how to make use of the knowledge from the past as preparation for an uncertain future.

All education deals with knowledge provided from past experiences because that is all we know. The only question is whether we should place our emphasis on the very recent past or the longer past. What happened yesterday, or even an hour ago, is already in the past; the present is only a knife edge between past and future. But while education is about the past, it is *for* the future — a future that is unknown but not totally unpredictable.

We can safely predict that both jobs and lifestyles will change, but there is much uncertainty about what kinds of jobs will be available in the twenty-first century. It seems certain that many job skills will become obsolete and that new skills will be required. Thirty years ago few predicted the large number of new jobs in computer science that would soon become available. At that time, very few people were trained for such jobs, but many who had strong backgrounds in mathematics and science were able to move into the jobs when they opened up. There will be comparable opportunities in the future for graduates who are broadly educated and hence able to move out in any of a number of different directions.

A Personal View

For the past quarter of a century, my personal view has been that a statement of the goal of education need be neither conservative nor progressive, neither a long list nor a short one — it can be made in a single sentence: *In a society of free men and women the proper goal of education is to prepare each individual to make wise independent decisions.* Educated persons are those who can choose between good and bad, truth and falsehood, the beautiful and the ugly, the worthwhile and the trivial. Education will help them to make ethical decisions, political decisions, decisions in the home and on the job. It will enable them to choose a good book, a good painting, a good piece of music. It will enable them to make the many decisions necessary in planning a good life and in conducting it properly.

To make such decisions, they will need a large fund of information but, even more important, they will need the ability to think clearly and logically about what they know — the ability to draw conclusions from evidence. The need for such information and for the ability to use it wisely should provide the basis for all educational planning.[12]

When this view of the goal of education first appeared in print in 1957, several reviewers reported that I was an existentialist. This was news to me, although it is true that existentialists stress decision making. My hope was that the statement of a single goal might provide a basis for reconciling some of the differences between progressives and conservatives, between liberal and vocational educators, and might be useful to curriculum makers and teachers.

---

1. Aristotle, *Politics*, bk. 8, chap. 1.
2. Stanley Elam, ed., *A Decade of Gallup Polls of Attitudes Toward Education, 1969-1978* (Bloomington, Ind.: Phi Delta Kappa, 1978).
3. Theodore C. Wagenaar, "High School Seniors' Views of Themselves and Their Schools: A Trend Analysis," *Phi Delta Kappan* 63 (September 1981): 31-32.
4. George Stoddard, "A New Design for The College of Liberal Arts and Sciences," *School and Society* 90 (1 May 1965).
5. Digest of Educational Statistics, NCES, U.S. Dept. of Ed., 1981, p. 166.
6. Lawrence Cremin, *The Transformation of the Schools* (New York: Alfred A. Knopf, 1961), p. vii.
7. R. M. Hutchins, Address at the 155th Convocation of the University of Chicago, 11 June 1929.

8. Arthur Bestor, *The Restoration of Learning* (New York: Alfred A. Knopf, 1952), pp. 8, 34.
9. *Harpers Magazine,* July 1954.
10. Fund for the Advancement of Education, *Annual Report,* 1957-59.
11. Norman Cousins, *Human Options* (New York: W. W. Norton & Co., 1981), p. 27.
12. Paul Woodring, *A Fourth of a Nation* (New York: McGraw-Hill, 1957), p. 111.

2

What Education Is Basic?

Although the term *basic education* has been used for a quarter of a century, it has not found its way into the dictionaries. The adjective *basic* is defined as "fundamental" or "providing a basis for." But for what? For life or for more education? Skill in conjugating Latin verbs is basic to a further study of Latin, but many Americans have lived good lives without it. Music is an essential part of the good life, but is not basic to further education.

To an American living in the twentieth century it seems obvious that teaching children to read is the most basic responsibility of the schools because literacy is essential both to good living and to further education. It might have seemed less obvious to Socrates. He used no textbooks, assigned no homework, and there is no evidence that he sent his students to libraries. He talked and, by asking the right questions, led his students to think rationally about the things that matter most. His method was the high point of the great oral tradition in education.

Much of the earliest literature — the *Iliad*, the *Odyssey*, and the *Vedic Hymns*, for example — was in verse, which made it easier to memorize. Alfred North Whitehead, in *Rhythm of Education*, says, "You cannot *read* Homer before you can read; but many a child, and in ages past many a man, has sailed with Odysseus over the seas of romance by the help of the spoken word of a mother or some wandering bard."

By the fifth and fourth centuries B.C., however, many Greeks had become literate. Aristotle wrote didactic prose and by his time many of his countrymen could read it.

In Rome, a few centuries later, literacy was common in the middle class; many read both Latin and Greek because many of the teachers were Greeks. Literacy was required of the large number of clerks and other civil servants. But we do not know what percentage of the total population was literate because the Romans did not think in statistical terms. (It would have been difficult with Roman numerals and no zero.) We do know that the great library at Alexandria, the greatest in the world until its destruction in 391 A.D. (by Christians who feared that pagan writing posed a threat to Biblical truth) housed thousands of manuscripts, which were available to those learned scholars who could read the various languages in which they were written.[1] Although the Romans had many books, their schools placed greater emphasis on oral rhetoric.

After the fall of Rome, literacy declined in Western Europe. The conviction that every person should learn to read did not take hold until the Protestants of the Reformation began to stress the importance of every Christian being able to read the Bible, and the advent of the printing press made many more books, including the Bible, available.

After the American Revolution, the Founding Fathers, notably Jefferson, Franklin, Madison, and Adams, were convinced that a self-governing nation required a literate electorate. They took steps to expand the system of public schools that had been started during the colonial period. Jefferson proposed a system of elementary, secondary, and higher education for Virginia. Even along the frontier, one-room schools began to appear. But universal literacy was still a long way off.

The census of 1870 reported that 11.5% of white Americans were still illiterate, as were 80% of the blacks (who were only a few years out of slavery). By 1900 these figures had been reduced to 44.5% for the blacks and 5% for the whites (only 3% for *native-born* whites). But these early censuses counted as literate anyone who *said* he could read and write. A more rigorous criterion would have resulted in a much higher percentage of illiterates.[2]

The census of 1980 reported that only one-half of one percent of all adults are illiterate, but census takers now assume that anyone with five years of schooling must be literate — a questionable assumption in schools that promote on an age basis regardless of achievement.[3]

Considerable confusion exists over the term "literacy;" it means different things to different people. At one end of the scale (the end apparently preferred by the Census Bureau) it means only the ability to write one's name and to read a few simple words. Others use the concept of "functional literacy," which is defined as the level that enables one to meet the practical needs of daily life. At the upper end of the scale are those who contend that anyone who prefers *Reader's Digest* to *Daedalus* is illiterate. At a conference on articulating secondary and higher education I once heard an indignant professor say that the freshmen in his class at Harvard were "illiterate," to which a high school teacher in the group aptly responded that the professor was demonstrating his own illiteracy by misusing the word.

The Reading Controversy

It is not true that the easier subjects should precede the harder. On the contrary, some of the hardest must come first because nature so dictates, and because they are essential to life. The first intellectual task which confronts an infant is the acquirement of spoken language. What an appalling task, the correlation of meaning with sounds! We all know that the infant does it, and that the miracle of his achievement is explicable. But so are all miracles, and yet to the wise they remain miracles.[4]

Alfred North Whitehead

Because the spoken language is acquired before the child comes to school, the most difficult task facing teachers is that of helping children learn to read — a task so formidable that first-grade teachers ought to be the most highly respected and best rewarded teachers of any grade level in school or college.

The oral tradition exemplified by Socrates is not sufficient today. Because a major part of our cultural heritage is transmitted through the printed page, because a self-governing nation needs an informed electorate, and because it is increasingly difficult for an illiterate adult to find employment or to live a good life in today's world, learning to read is widely accepted as the proper first step in formal education. All schools accept this responsibility; all educators agree that it is essential, and yet the teaching of reading — the methods used and the results achieved — has engendered one of the most rancorous debates in twentieth-century American education.

Although the debate had been smouldering for a long time, it came to widespread attention in 1955 with the publication of *Why Johnny Can't Read* by Rudolph Flesch, a "consultant on readability" to various corporations and press services, who has a Ph.D. from Teachers College, Columbia University. This book took the country by storm. Although it received sharply critical reviews in professional journals and was dismissed by most educators as a diatribe, it received enthusiastic reviews in magazines read by the general public. It was serialized in many newspapers. Tens of thousands of parents seized upon it, and their purchases kept it on the best-seller list for 30 weeks. Because many of the readers were intelligent, well-educated people, it was widely discussed by school boards, in parents meetings, in legislative committees, and in various conferences on education. Its popularity reflected widespread discontent; it became obvious that many parents agreed with Flesch that there was something wrong with the way reading was being taught and that they were determined to do something about it. Whether or not

Flesch was correct, it was obvious that educators could not ignore evidence of such widespread concern.

Flesch's thesis was that there had been a dramatic decline in children's reading ability in "recent" years and that this decline could be attributed entirely to the decline in the use of phonics in the schools. His remedy was simple: teach phonics rigorously and drop all other methods. If the school will not do it, the parents should do it themselves; and Flesch was eager to show them how. The fact that his was a "how-to-do-it" book — the full title was *Why Johnny Can't Read and What You Can do About It* — undoubtedly helped to make it a best seller.

Educators, including reading specialists, responded that there is no one best way to teach reading — that phonics should be included but only as a part of a total program and not necessarily as the first step. Nila Banton Smith, former president of the International Reading Association, was quoted as saying that some children "aren't ready for concentrated teaching of phonics until the third or fourth grade."[5] (It was not until a decade later that some reading specialists reversed this stand and took the position that phonics is important *only* in the beginning and a waste of time after that.) And most educators denied that there had been a decline in reading ability.

But the debate continued. In 1961 Charles Walcutt edited a book titled *Tomorrow's Illiterates*, with an introduction by Jacques Barzun and seven essays discussing "the growing illiteracy of American children."[6]

When I wrote an editorial on the reading controversy for *Saturday Review* in January 1962, we received requests for 50,000 reprints — far more than we had received for reprints on any other subject. Obviously, many people still were concerned about the problem.

In 1967 Jeanne Chall, director of the Reading Laboratory at Harvard, published her report of a comprehensive survey of the literature on the teaching of reading from 1910 to 1965.[7] Although her book was more scholarly than Flesch's and was intended more for educators than for the general public, she also came to the conclusion that phonics is essential for beginners and should be introduced into the program early. Unlike Flesch, she did not contend that it should be the only method used.

What are the facts? I am not a reading specialist and have read only a small part of the voluminous literature on the subject, but if I may borrow a line from a familiar document, "We hold these truths to be self-evident":

1. The great *majority* of children in school today are learning to read. If "Johnny" is taken to mean the average or typical American child (and many readers did interpret it that way), the charge that Johnny can't read is arrant nonsense. He can and he does.

2. A substantial *minority* go through school without learning to read well enough to satisfy their teachers, their parents, their future employers, or themselves. The size of this minority depends on the criteria used.

3. Inability to read constitutes a more serious problem in today's world

than it did in yesterday's simpler society. This fact makes the nonreader more conspicuous.

4. The number of poor readers or nonreaders who enter — and occasionally graduate from — high schools has increased over the years, not because of a growing number of illiterates in the age group but because more schools now use social promotion without regard to academic talent or achievement.

Some other facts, though not self-evident, are supported by the evidence. The problems faced by beginners differ substantially from those of mature readers whose eyes move rapidly across the page while grasping the meaning of whole words and paragraphs. To beginners, many words are unfamiliar. They need a code for deciphering them.

A reader with a knowledge of phonics can easily pronounce new words such as *Tildustar* or *Polyruckstan*, but having pronounced them does this reader know their meaning? A reader who knows phonics may still have trouble with words such as *ocean, tongue*, or *cough*, and would never guess from a knowledge of phonics that *Cairo*, Illinois, is not pronounced like *Cairo*, Egypt; that the pronunciation of *Lima*, Ohio, differs from that of *Lima*, Peru; or that *Thames* and *Spokane* are not pronounced in accordance with common phonetic rules. There is widespread disagreement concerning the percentage of English words that are not spelled and pronounced according to phonic rules; Flesch says only 2½%, other estimates range up to 80%, and most reading specialists offer estimates somewhere between these extremes. But there are enough exceptions to phonetic pronunciation to make problems for any reader.

Older people who say, "When I was young, all children learned to read" either have poor memories, were unaware of the deficiencies of some of their classmates, or attended selective private schools that evade the problem of educating slow learners by not admitting them. There have always been many poor readers, no matter what methods were used.

It is inevitable that some children will read better than their parents; some less well. Parents of the children who read less well are likely to be critical of the schools. An adult who now reads easily is likely to forget how hard it was to *learn* to read. To put yourself in the place of a child who has not yet learned, try reading this sentence:

.ɘɔnɘɈnɘƨ ɘlqmiƨ ƨiʜɈ bɒɘɿ oɈ Ɉlυɔiʇʇib ylɘmɘɿɈxɘ Ɉi bniʇ yɒm υoY

To a beginner, ordinary print seems as incomprehensible as does this mirror image. A reader's first problem is to recognize and pronounce individual words. For this, a knowledge of phonics is helpful *when* reading a phonic language, as is English for the most part, though with many exceptions. (Phonics would be useless for reading Chinese, Japanese, or Korean, because the characters used in these languages represent ideas or objects rather than sounds.) The next task is to get the meaning of the sentence; phonics is of little help in that.

It is also necessary for the reader to know whether the sentence is read from left to right or from right to left (as is true of some languages), whether the page is read from top to bottom or from bottom to top, and whether the book is read from front to back or from back to front (also true of some languages). A child may, like the boy in Kipling's story *Kim*, wonder whether one reads the black or the white part of the page.

Fashions in teaching methodology go in cycles. From the 1920s until the 1950s reading specialists, with the support of one wing of the progressive movement, deemphasized phonics because of their conviction that learning the meaning of words was more important and should come first. In some schools phonics was almost completely ignored. I recall asking the teachers in a summer-school class — sometime in the early Fifties — whether there was any truth to the charge that they taught no phonics. One first-grade teacher replied, "Oh, we teach phonics, but we have to sneak it in because it is contrary to accepted policy."

Flesch was on firm ground in saying that phonics should come into the program early. He was right in thinking, at the time he was writing *Why Johnny Can't Read*, that phonics was being neglected in many schools as reflected in the programs and books produced by some of the reading specialists of that day. If he had said that much and then stopped, his book would have had greater influence on teachers, because many of them agreed.

But he did not stop. He insisted that phonics is the only way to teach reading and should be the foundation of the total program — a view which teachers could not accept. By his choice of title for his book he gave many readers the impression that *most* children were not learning to read. This was far from true. And he alienated teachers by implying that most teachers of reading were incompetent. They were not.

He also used a faulty and incomplete definition of *reading*. This is made clear by his anecdote of a personal experience. "Many years ago . . . I took a semester's course in Czech; I have forgotten everything about the language itself, but I still remember how the letters are pronounced, plus the simple rule that all words have the accent on the first syllable. Armed with this knowledge, I once surprised a native of Prague by reading aloud from a Czech newspaper. 'Oh, you know Czech?' he asked. 'No, I don't understand a word of it,' I answered. 'I can only read it.'"[8]

No teacher, and no sensible parent, is likely to agree that pronouncing words without understanding what they mean is really reading. It is only one step in reading.

Since about 1960 there has been a gradual shift back toward decoding words, with a phonics emphasis. Flesch deserves credit for arousing public interest in the problem, but Chall deserves more credit for convincing educators of the need for change. Flesch's book was designed more to inflame emotions than to persuade educators; Chall's book offered better evidence, and her tone was quietly persuasive. She was not alone, of course; other reading specialists were moving in the same direction.

Today nearly all reading programs provide instruction in phonics — perhaps not as much as Flesch would like but probably as much as the children need, *if* they learn what is included in the program. Inevitably, some do not. The programs used in the 1980s also emphasize reading for meaning — as they should.

No matter what methods are employed, there are, and always have been, special problems to be dealt with in teaching children with reading and learning disabilities. These children must be dealt with individually. Merely giving them more phonics will not solve their problems.

Fears have been expressed repeatedly that Americans have become, or are about to become, less literate and less interested in reading. At the turn of the century, *Publishers Weekly*, the book industry's trade journal, warned that the rising popularity of bicycling and baseball would result in a drastic decline in reading. In the Twenties, fears were expressed that the popularity of motion pictures and radio would have that effect. Since the Fifties, many have feared that television would distract children from books. It certainly appears to have done so for many children; yet books are selling better than ever before.

No one can say with confidence whether there has been an improvement or a decline in reading skills over the last two or three generations because we have no reliable evidence, based on nationwide samples, of the reading ability of our ancestors. Recent nationwide surveys seem to give evidence of improvement in reading skills during the last decade on the part of children in the elementary grades but no improvement, and apparently some decline, on the part of high school students.

But the much maligned "Johnny" can read, and frequently does.

The Second R

The area in which a poor education shows up first is in self-expression, oral or written. It makes little difference how many university courses or degrees a person may own. If he cannot use words to move an idea from one point to another, his education is incomplete. The business of assembling the right words, putting them down in proper sequence, enabling each one to pull its full weight in the conveyance of meaning — these are the essentials. [9]

Norman Cousins

Writing . . . is the only subject for which the U.S National Assessment of Education has shown a consistent decline. [10]

Ralph Tyler

It would be a forward step if we could agree to let the second R stand for rhetoric — the art of speaking or writing effectively. Writing, or *'ritin'*, as the word was used by those who coined the slogan "teach the three R's," meant only penmanship. Legible penmanship still is necessary, but the interest in beautiful penmanship, with all the flourishes, has declined since the invention of the typewriter. Indeed, it could be argued that typing has become one of the basics.

Those who charge that the second R is neglected today do not mean penmanship but rather skill in putting thoughts on paper. Some have attributed the neglect of writing to the replacement of essay tests by objective tests, but essay tests were never a good way of teaching students to write well because there is never time during the examination hour for careful thought or for the rewriting and revision that good writing requires. Much more serious is the fact that today's teachers in both school and college probably assign fewer papers than were assigned 50 years ago. (I say "probably" only because no one has made a nationwide count, but I have no real doubt about it.)

Whatever the reason, the writing skills of today's graduates leave much to be desired. Regulations written by government bureaucrats are full of jargon, unclear in meaning. Laws are written in such clumsy fashion that courts cannot agree on their intent. Recent U.S. Presidents find it necessary to employ speech writers to help them put their thoughts into English. They defend this practice by saying that they are "too busy," forgetting that Abraham Lincoln, in the midst of war, was not too busy to compose the Gettysburg Address, nor was Winston Churchill too busy to write some of his best speeches during the Battle of Britain. These men understood the importance of effective communication. And they wrote better than any hired speech writer.

Members of Congress today neither write nor speak with the clarity of a Clay, Webster, or Calhoun — Adlai Stevenson was probably the last to do so. State legislators are even worse. Reporters covering the activities of the Michigan State Legislature reported the following gems, each intoned by a different elected official:

"There comes a time to put principles aside and do what's right."

"From now on I'm watching everything you do with a fine toothed comb."

"This bill goes to the very heart of the moral fiber of human anatomy."

"We've got them right where they want us."

"I'm not only for capital punishment. I'm also for the preservation of life."

"Some of our friends want it in the bill, some of our friends want it out, and Jerry and I are going to stick with our friends."

"Mr. Speaker, what bill did we just pass?"

(Wall Street Journal, 19 March 1982)

But let us not be too quick to place all the blame on the *public* schools. Many state legislators are graduates of "the best private schools," as are some of the bureaucrats who persist in saying "at this point in time" when they mean "now." Most legislators and recent presidents have degrees from colleges or universities; all of them are mature men or women who have had ample opportunity, since leaving school, to read widely and to learn to think, speak, and write more clearly if they had the will. Schools can accept only a small portion of the responsibility.

But we should do our part. All teachers, whether of English, science, physical education, or industrial arts, can help by demonstrating their own ability to think logically and to speak and write with clarity and force. In universities, the teachers of teachers can make their contribution by making sure that those who lack such ability do not become teachers of any subject at any level.

When I was teaching high school English, we often required students to write themes of 1,000, 2,000, or 5,000 words. Usually they did not have that much to say about the topic assigned so they padded to fill the space. Inevitably, this led to bad writing.

My view of how writing should be taught has been altered by my experience as a writer and editor. As a writer I have often been asked to review a book in "not more than 1,200 words" or to write an entry for an encyclopedia in "not more than 200 (or 1,000 or 2,000) words." Because I have far more to say, I find it necessary to condense, to leave out less important things, to omit unnecessary words. As an editor I often found it necessary to ask a writer to rewrite a manuscript of 5,000 words in half that many while saying the same things. This was partly because of limited space, but I also knew that if the writer reduced the length of the manuscript, it would be tightened up and superfluous parts would be eliminated. This nearly always resulted in clearer and more forceful writing.

As a result of this experience I now ask students to write shorter papers, not longer ones. If I were teaching composition in a public school today, I would assign a topic, or let the students select one, and then ask them to write as *briefly* as possible. I would give the highest grades to the shortest papers *if* they covered the subject well.

The task of the teacher is not to produce writers of great literature — no one knows how to do that — it is to develop citizens who can speak and write clearly and effectively. To achieve this end I would ask elementary school students to explain as briefly as possible how a game such as baseball, checkers, or dominoes is played. The students would be told that their readers understand English but know nothing about the game and want to learn to play it. The writers will not be present when their instructions are read; therefore, they will have to define terms, describe the objects used in the game, and explain the rules so that they give their readers all the necessary information about the game. To check the clarity of their writing, they might show their instructions to someone unfamiliar with the game and ask if that person understands how to play it after reading the instructions.

Or children might be asked to explain the differences between a dog and a cat in terms that would be understandable to someone who had never seen either. Or they could be asked to distinguish between an elm tree and an oak or between the climate of Ohio and California. In the latter case, they would quickly discover that the real difference is not that California is warmer but that its climate is more varied — some parts of California can be colder than Ohio. In learning to write clearly, one must think clearly, must learn when generalizations are appropriate and when they are not.

At the secondary level we might ask students to explain the differences between a novel and a short story, between a president and a prime minister, or between an atom and a molecule. We might ask them to explain how an airplane flies. In writing such papers they would, of course, learn a great deal about science and other subjects, while at the same time learning to express themselves clearly.

This, of course, is not the way one learns to write a poem or a novel. But it is the kind of writing most needed today and the kind students will use all of their lives, whether they write a memo to the boss, an explanation for their employees, or a note to the newsboy explaining that they do not want the paper delivered while they are away on vacation but would like to have one on the day of their return. Expository writing is *basic* education.

The Third R

Because mathematics is the language of science, our nation needs a large number of men and women who have a sophisticated knowledge of higher mathematics. But anyone planning to become a scientist, engineer, statistician, or computer programmer needs more than the elementary mathematics properly called *basic*. After learning the basics students need advanced, specialized mathematics that builds upon the basics.

Basic mathematics is that needed by *all* who live in today's world, whether they are farmers, poets, housewives, clerks, philosophers, plumbers, or those who work on assembly lines. Because the Internal Revenue Service has made us a nation of bookkeepers, everyone must keep an account of income, expenditures, and contributions to charity. Every American faces the problems of balancing a checkbook, keeping a budget, and computing taxes. Those who cook find it necessary to convert ounces, cups, and tablespoonfuls into grams and liters. Because we vote on bond issues it is necessary to know how much three mils per thousand dollars evaluation will add to our taxes. Soon we may need to know whether a predicted temperature of 15 degrees Celsius means we need our topcoats and whether a highway speed of 95 kilometers per hour violates the 55-mile-per hour speed limit.

Everyone needs some conception of distances, dimensions, magnitudes, and quantities. If we wish to compare the height of the Himalayas with that of the Andes it is of no great help to be told that one range "towers to the skies" while the peaks of the other are "lost in the clouds." When we learn that Mt.

Everest has an elevation of 29,028 feet above sea level but that the elevation of Aconcagua is 22,834 feet, we have the answer. Understanding the relative value of the two numbers is basic mathematics.

Does a lot measuring 50 by 150 feet have room for a garden? Will a carport 16 by 22 feet house our two cars? Will a house with 1,700 square feet of floor space meet our family needs? Does a bedroom measuring 10 by 12 feet have room for a kingsize bed? If a city is 400 miles away, can we reach it in a day's drive? Will a car with a 1.6 litre engine pull a trailer? Does a birthrate of 15 per thousand lead to a population explosion? If we buy a house for $70,000 and pay for it with a thirty-year mortgage at 12%, what is the real cost? How much damage can we expect from a wind velocity of 75 miles per hour or from an earthquake measuring 7.2 on the Richter Scale? Does the fact that Iran has an area of 636,000 square miles mean that it is about the size of Ohio, Texas, Alaska, or the entire United States? When we read that the Falkland Islands have an area of 6,418 square miles, does that mean they are about the size of Long Island, Nantucket, Santa Catalina, Orcas, or some other island with which we are familiar?

The mathematics that is basic for living in twentieth and twenty-first century America includes:
1. Computational skills: addition, subtraction, multiplication and division of whole numbers, fractions, and decimals. (Using hand-held calculators when appropriate.)
2. The ability to estimate size, distance, quantity, and weight, using both standard and metric measurement, and the ability to convert each into the other.
3. Problem solving as applied to everyday situations.
4. The ability to read and interpret tables, charts, and graphs that appear in newspapers and magazines.
5. Some minimal understanding of statistics such as the ability to differentiate between mean and median, understanding of percentages, and awareness that high correlation does not mean certainty of prediction.
6. An introduction to computers.

The National Council of Supervisors of Mathematics proposes a list similar to this but adds the ability to *construct* charts, graphs, and tables, as well as the use of mathematics for prediction and probability. As I see it, however, these go beyond basic mathematics and into the higher level.

By the end of middle school a child of normal intelligence should have competency in *basic* mathematics. This leaves ample time during the high school years for a firm grounding in the mathematics that goes beyond the basics, and builds upon them, for those who will need it for their further education or for their vocations.

But What Else Is Basic?

The present back-to-basics movement resembles what was called "essentialism" a half century ago — a movement led by William Bagley of Teachers College, Columbia University, in a futile effort to stem the drift toward progressivism. The essentialist's position, as stated by Bagley, was that the schools should:

> . . . prepare boys and girls for adult responsibilities through systematic training in such subjects as reading, writing, arithmetic, history, and English, requiring mastery of such subjects, and when necessary, stressing discipline and obedience, with informal learning recognized but regarded as supplementary rather than central. [12]

Although this sounded like plain common sense to many parents, Bagley gained few followers among educational leaders of his day, for a strong tide was running against him. He found himself described by fellow educators as "conservative," "reactionary," or "old-fashioned." In the 1920s and 1930s these adjectives were enough to drive any movement up against the wall. But with the decline of progressive education in the 1950s — and especially after the launching of Sputnik — essentialism returned in a different guise and with a new slogan.

Some of those who urge a return to basic education today would restrict it to the three R's, but even the much maligned one-room country schools of the nineteenth century taught much more than that. Their curriculum included instruction in spelling, history, geography, physiology, and civil government. Teachers in those schools were also advised to "cultivate in children a love of country, beauty and truth, improve their manners, and above all raise their moral standards to make them worthy of their great nation." [13]

Children of normal intelligence can learn to read, write, and perform basic mathematical calculations in three or four years, just as their ancestors did. What, then, should be the curriculum of the middle school and high school? It is obviously not sufficient for children and adolescents to spend all 12 years of schooling on further mastering of these three basic skills.

It can well be argued that other subjects of instruction are desirable for all and essential for some without properly being called "basic." Such a distinction might help to clear the air. The Council for Basic Education (CBE), a national organization that has played a conspicuous role for some years in encouraging basic education, proposes a definition of basic that includes most of the academic subjects traditionally taught in secondary school: history, English, mathematics, science, and foreign languages. Because of its widespread influence with legislatures and school boards, and because many professional educators have been prone to ignore its influence, this seems an appropriate place for some observations on the history of the Council for Basic Education.

The 10 men responsible for founding it had one thing in common: As individuals, they spoke out vigorously, often stridently, against the educational trends of the 1950s, including many that could be loosely grouped under the term "progressive education." They were scornful of "teachers colleges" and denounced "professors of education." In return they were denounced by professional educators. They discovered that most of the professional education journals were closed to them, and when they wrote for popular magazines the editors were threatened by educators with mass cancellation of subscriptions. They had been called "enemies of the schools," but as they saw it and as they deeply believed, they were not enemies at all but the best defenders of sound education for American youth.

CBE was launched in 1956 with 134 charter members who, in addition to the 10 founding members, included many distinguished scholars: Crane Brinton, Joseph Wood Krutch, Allan Nevins, Mark Van Doren, Louis Hacker, Stewart Cairns, William Ernest Hocking, Richard Hofstader, and Howard Mumford Jones, to mention only a few. This is an impressive list, but it is notable that among the 134 there were only a few natural scientists, very few elementary or secondary teachers, and only a half dozen psychologists and educators. The great majority of the charter members were university professors of literature or history.

This self-selection influenced the tone of their writing. When CBE spokesmen wrote about the humanities they were on familiar ground and their writing was sophisticated. But when they expressed their views concerning the processes of learning and of teaching they seemed much less sophisticated. They seemed to believe that all courses in "education" dealt exclusively with methodology and they were contemptuous of methodology. But they were not consistent about this. CBE vigorously stressed the importance of phonics as the solution to the reading problem, and phonics is obviously a method of teaching reading — one that must be learned in professional courses.

In its first policy statement CBE proposed to initiate and support measures to ensure:

1. That all students without exception receive adequate instruction in the basic intellectual disciplines, especially English, mathematics, science, history, and foreign languages;

2. That the fullest opportunity is afforded to students of high ability to reach mature levels of achievement without waste of time;

3. That clear standards of actual accomplishment are used to measure each student's progress and to govern promotion to higher levels of the educational system;

4. That teachers are thoroughly educated in the subjects they teach and in current developments therein;

5. That vocational training is offered in due subordination to the school's fundamental purpose of intellectual discipline, and that standards of achievement are maintained as rigorously in vocational as in academic fields;

6. That school administrators are encouraged and supported in resisting pressures to divert school time to activities of minor educational significance, to curricula overemphasizing social adjustment at the expense of intellectual discipline, and to programs that call upon the school to assume responsibilities properly belonging to the home, to religious bodies, and other agencies.

The phrase in the first paragraph, "all students without exception," suggests that the writers were unaware of the total range of individual differences in learning capacity. No doubt they were. Many of the humanistic scholars in CBE had never had even a first course in psychology and had never tried teaching in a public school where children of all levels of intellectual talent were present. Apart from that, the pronouncement might have been acceptable to a substantial number of teachers and other professional educators, who also wanted to establish standards and to resist pressures to add still more responsibilities to those which the schools had already accepted.

But CBE alienated even "conservative" educators by their expressions of contempt for "educationists" and their scorn of "teachers colleges." Teachers knew, even though CBE apparently did not, that the teachers college as a separate, single-purpose institution was rapidly disappearing from the scene and that most teachers were being educated in liberal arts colleges or universities. Those who had attended teachers colleges knew that the statement often made by CBE leaders, "teachers colleges teach nothing but methods," was utter nonsense, that teachers colleges have always given instruction in the academic disciplines and that many courses in "education" deal with educational philosophy and educational psychology rather than with methods.

Writing in 1960 Myron Lieberman described CBE as "a conglomeration of viewers with alarm" and "a kind of Progressive Education Association for educational conservatives." He predicted that it would "orbit aimlessly in space for a few decades and then wither away, claiming the widespread acceptance of its platform as the reason for its dissolution." Other educators, particularly those of a progressive persuasion, had still harsher things to say. But CBE has refused to wither away.

A major reason for its success in gaining adherents was the monthly CBE *Bulletin* (now called *Basic Education*), which for many years was edited by Mortimer Smith, an urbane and witty gadfly who was skillful at deflating pomposity, exposing plausible nonsense, and illuminating some of the dark recesses of education. His ironic comments attracted the interest of so many well-educated parents, school board members, legislators, and the press, that he will deserve some mention in future histories of twentieth-century education, even though he has never been popular with professional educators.[14]

Although Smith's was the most persistent voice of CBE, he was not its best known polemicist. For a time that distinction fell on historian Arthur Bestor, author of *Educational Wastelands, The Restoration of Learning,* and numerous articles in which he excoriated the group he called "educationists" and urged a return to solid academic scholarship in the schools. After the launching of Sputnik in 1957, many more writers turned their attention to education. One educator remarked, "People who had been ignoring the schools for years suddenly went into orbit and started beeping."

The most penetrating beeps came from an admiral named Rickover who used his prestige as father of the atomic submarine as a platform from which to launch his views on education — views that were heard by congressional committees on education and printed in the *Congressional Record.* Bestor wryly remarked that just as he was becoming accustomed to being the favorite target for educationists, the barrage against him stopped suddenly as all the big guns were turned on Rickover. CBE welcomed Rickover with open arms.

Over the years, CBE gradually modified some of its more extreme views, as any reader of the monthly CBE *Bulletin* will discover. In its robust youth its spokesmen were prone to make categorical statements beginning, "All children, without exception, *must* . . ." but as the years passed they learned that individual differences really do exist and are so great in magnitude that it is impossible to hold all children to the same standards. At first CBE placed the blame for poor teaching squarely and almost exclusively on professors of education, but eventually they learned that most teachers of the academic subjects received their instruction in those subjects not from professors of education but from university professors in the various disciplines. In time, some CBE spokesmen modified their view of teacher education to the point where it was possible for them to admit that a scholarly knowledge of the subject may not be *all* that a teacher needs — that there is a place for professional education.

During these same years many educators have moved at least a few steps in the direction of CBE. Now they talk less about trying to meet the needs of the "whole child" and more about the importance of teaching the fundamentals of the academic disciplines. Educators today are also more willing than they were in 1956 to support standards for advancement and for graduation. Consequently, the gulf between CBE and professors of education is not nearly so deep as it once was. Today it is entirely possible for professional educators to support and defend basic education without deviating from their conviction that schools must also go beyond the basics and include other subjects and other activities in the curriculum.

In spite of its early limitations, CBE has played a useful role. It stressed the importance of the academic disciplines at a time when such an emphasis was badly needed. It gave encouragement to the many secondary teachers who are firmly committed to scholarly learning. It called attention to trivia in the curriculum and contributed to the establishment of educational priorities. It helped to stiffen the backbone of school board members who had identified weaknesses in the school but had been intimidated by the expertise of educators. And it forced professional educators to reexamine their own position. For a small and poorly financed organization, these were no mean achievements.

It appears to me, however, that the Council for Basic Education was misnamed. It could more appropriately have called itself the Council for Liberal Education in the Public Schools. The curriculum they propose goes well beyond the basics and into the secondary level of education.

The back-to-basics movement is currently in a state of disarray because *basic* has come to mean different things to different people. In 1977 the Gallup Poll asked, "Have you heard or read about the back-to-basics movement?" Of those who answered in the affirmative, 83% said they favored the movement. But when asked what it meant, the responses of the majority indicated that they think of the term in relation to certain values as well as to the three R's. *Basics*, to many of the respondents, means "good manners," "politeness," "respect for teachers," "obedience," "respect for elders," "structured classrooms," and "back to the old ways of teaching."

The meaning does not appear to be much clearer to educators. When a group of educators met in Racine, Wisconsin, in 1977 to examine the state of the basic skills in American education, the topics first discussed included the basic skills of learning; but before the conference concluded the participants were discussing almost everything that has ever been proposed as an educational objective: "the use of leisure," "positive self-concepts," "economic capability," "health," "direct contact, and if possible, involvement with power structures and social forces," and "the will to do something about the problems that affect our lives, families, neighborhoods, and larger communities."[15]

If all these objectives are *basic* the adjective has no meaning; we may just as well say *education* without the adjective. Since the correct use of English language is obviously basic let us again check the dictionary for help with a definition. *Basic* means "fundamental," "providing a base for," or "serving as a starting point." It does not mean everything that someone considers useful, desirable, or valuable. Unless we can agree on the definition of *basic* the back-to-basics movement is a meaningless concept.

Is Foreign Language a Basic?

In its first statement of policy the Council for Basic Education listed foreign language as one of the basics. Mortimer Adler, in his *Paideia Proposal*, agrees, as do many of those who are demanding more emphasis on basics in the schools.

This reflects a long tradition. From Roman times until the eighteenth or early nineteenth centuries, Latin was the language of scholarship. Few scholarly tomes were written in the vernaculars, with the result that a student who knew only the language spoken in his own country was not prepared for higher education. In the "grammar schools" the language taught was Latin, often supplemented by Greek.

After most of the classics had been translated into the vernaculars, and more scholars began writing in their native languages, teachers of the classical languages defended the need for their services by proclaiming that a study of Latin "strengthens the mind" and hence was good preparation for the study of other subjects.

As a result of the research of educational psychologists in the twentieth century, the view that Latin has some special "mind strengthening" value fell into disrepute. Many colleges began accepting modern languages instead of Latin and Greek as requirements for admission. By the second half of this century, the less selective colleges began admitting students who had received no instruction in any language other than English. Some colleges also dropped foreign languages from their lists of requirements for the bachelor's degree. As a result, the number of high school students electing a foreign language declined sharply.

It is true that Americans are notably deficient in foreign languages when compared with Europeans. Educated Americans who travel abroad are often embarrassed to find that while they speak the languages of the countries they visit haltingly, if at all, the people of these countries speak English. The lack of emphasis on foreign languages in the schools is not the only reason for this. A more significant reason is that most Americans have little opportunity to use a second language outside of school. Europeans, because of the geographical proximity of nations, have more opportunity to use other languages in their daily lives. When students in an American classroom ask for the salt in good French, they get an "A". In a European home or restaurant they get the salt. Such reinforcement makes it much more likely that the European student will remember the word, while an American can safely forget it as soon as the grades are in.

One way to encourage American students to elect foreign languages is to offer better instruction. In the past, language study has often been a deadly chore, but in some American schools the quality of teaching has improved substantially within the past 30 years. In these schools an effort is made to enable the student to function *within* the foreign language rather than to place the emphasis on translating it into English.

Today it is difficult to find enough young Americans to fill overseas posts that require a speaking and written knowledge of additional languages. Knowledge of more than one language is essential for anyone planning to undertake advanced study in literature, history, or other humanities and is valuable for those who will become scholars in other fields. But it is difficult to know which languages to teach — no school can teach them all.

In my own lifetime I have lived and worked in places where the primary language of the people around me was Japanese, Tagalog, and Melanesian Pidgeon, my need for which could not have been predicted when I was a student. Latin is no longer the language of scholarship; French is no longer the language of diplomacy. It is doubtful that French and German are now the most valuable languages for candidates for the Ph.D. in science or the social sciences.

Clearly there is need for more and better language instruction in American schools, but to say that foreign language is basic *"for all students without exception"* is to stretch the definition of *basic*. It is true that even slow learners can learn to speak a second language about as well as they speak English, *if* given plenty of time to learn it and the motivation to use it on a daily basis. But if all public school students who still are having difficulty with English, arithmetic, and other basic skills were to spend enough school time on foreign languages to become proficient, it would be time subtracted from that they now spend on basic subjects they sorely need.

Foreign language is essential for many, valuable for others, but cannot be considered basic for all American students. Other subjects have higher priority.

Is Geography a Basic?

Of all the school subjects, geography is the most neglected in American schools. Few students study it in either high school or college, and what they learn in middle school or junior high (where it is sometimes lost in a social studies course) is clearly insufficient. Yet no one seems interested in promoting it. The Council for Basic Education does not include it in its list of basics. Conferences on basic education rarely give it more than a passing mention. Only half of all U.S. colleges offer geography courses, and the majority of these have only one or two faculty members in geography. In 1982 the University of Michigan decided to eliminate its geography department entirely, and the dean of arts and sciences at the University of Pittsburgh has called for closing the department of geography there. Departments elsewhere are reported high on the "hit list" for retrenchment.[16]

Yet a knowledge of the landscapes, climates, boundaries, peoples, animals, plants, and other resources of the various continents, islands, nations, and states is basic to the study of history, political science, economics, geology, biology, and many other disciplines. It is also basic preparation for living in, understanding, and moving about in today's world.

Some men in high government office seem hazy even about the location of nations. Older readers may recall press reports of a man appointed as ambassador to a South American nation who, in his Senate hearing, could not locate that nation on the map and did not know what language was spoken there.

No child should be allowed to leave the eighth grade (and no one should be granted a driver's license) without being able to read a map. Yet military schools find it necessary to give officers basic instruction in map reading, even though most of the candidates are college graduates. During World War II, I left San Francisco on a troopship bound for an unannounced destination. On the third day out we were told that we were going to New Guinea. I was traveling as one of a group of Information-Education officers, most of whom had master's or doctor's degrees, yet many of them had no idea where New Guinea was or what it was. Though we were headed in a southwesterly direction over the Pacific, some thought New Guinea was in Africa, others said South America.

New Guinea, as we soon learned, is a huge island — the second largest on our planet. Its area is greater than that of California, Oregon, and Washington combined. It extends so far from west to east that if the northwest tip were placed over Seattle the southeast end — Milne Bay for which we were headed — would be over Kansas City. And although it is not far south of the equator, it has snow-capped mountains as well as rain forests, swamps, and upland meadows. This island was to be part of our lives — some of my friends are buried there — but our schools had left us totally ignorant of it.

More recent international conflicts have revealed our ignorance of Korea, Vietnam, Saudi Arabia, the West Bank, Jordan, Syria, Afghanistan, and the Falkland Islands. On a cruise ship crossing the Indian Ocean last winter, I was asked by a passenger whether the land mass silhouetted against the sunset ahead of us was South America. She was a Wellesley graduate.

A comprehensive knowledge of world geography can be gained in half or a third the time it takes to learn a single foreign language. The basic geography appropriate as part of the required public school curriculum can be understood by nearly all students — by many who cannot be expected to understand calculus, chemistry, the plays of Shakespeare, or the poetry of Milton and Yeats. Geography provides the kind of information that is necessary for traveling, or for reading the daily paper or a newsmagazine, or for understanding the weather report on television.

Regardless of the grade level, it is easy for a good teacher who knows the subject to arouse student interest. All that is needed are some good books, many pictures, a globe, and many maps — not just political maps but relief maps, geological maps, population maps, and maps showing wind and sea currents, climates, and the distribution of animals, vegetation, and other natural resources. Of course, the teacher, too, must understand maps as well as books.

In preparing teachers for this subject, the old-time normal schools and single-purpose teachers colleges did a better job than is being done in today's graduate schools of education. In normal schools, everyone planning to teach in an elementary school had a solid course in world geography. Today it is possible in some states to be certified for teaching all subjects up through the eighth grade without a single course in geography.

I do not know the reason for this neglect, but I am confident that it could easily be repaired. For anyone who wants to restore the basics, geography is a good place to start.

1. *Encyclopaedia Britannica*, Macropaedia, s.v. "Censorship."
2. *Historical Statistics of the U.S. to 1957*. U.S. Dept. of Commerce, Bureau of the Census.
3. *Statistical Abstract of the U.S.*, (1981), p. 143.
4. Alfred North Whitehead, *The Aims of Education and Other Essays*, Mentor Books (New York: Macmillan, 1929), pp. 27-28.
5. Mortimer Smith, "The Reading Problem," *American Scholar* (Summer 1969):434.
6. Charles Walcutt, *Tomorrow's Illiterates* (Boston: Little, Brown & Co., 1961).
7. Jeanne Chall, *Learning to Read: The Great Debate* (New York: McGraw-Hill, 1967). *See also* Jeanne Chall, *Reading 1967-1977: A Decade of Change and Promise*, Fastback 97 (Bloomington, Ind.: Phi Delta Kappa, 1977).
8. Rudolph Flesch, *Why Johnny Can't Read* (New York: Harper & Row, 1955), p. 23.
9. Norman Cousins, *Human Options* (New York: W.W. Norton & Co., 1981), p. 32.
10. Ralph Tyler, "The U.S. vs. the World: A Comparison of Educational Performance," *Phi Delta Kappan* 62 (January 1981):307-10.
11. *Digest of Education Statistics*, NCES, U.S. Govt. Printing Office, 1981, p. 210.
12. Edgar Knight, *Fifty Years of American Education* (New York: Ronald Press, 1952), p. 273.
13. Wayne Fuller, *The Old Country School* (Chicago: The University of Chicago Press, 1982).
14. For a collection of Mortimer Smith's essays see his book, *A Decade of Comment on Education* (Washington, D.C.: CBE, 1966).
15. Ben Brodinsky, *Defining the Basics of American Education*, Fastback 95 (Bloomington, Ind.: Phi Delta Kappa, 1977), pp. 32-36.
16. The *Chronicle of Higher Education*, 26 May 1982, p. 1.

3

What Values and Beliefs Shall Be Taught?

All men do not honor the same virtue, so they naturally hold different opinions in regard to training in virtue.

Aristotle

Concerning the Gods, there are those who deny the very existence of the Godhead; others say that it exists but concerns itself only with great and heavenly matters, not with individuals on earth. . . . Still others are those who cry, I move not without thy knowledge.

Epictetus

Some of the most persistent educational problems reflect the great diversity among Americans in religious beliefs, values, and morals. If we all accepted the moral code that was widely taught (though not always observed) in the 1890s, we might agree that courses in sex do not belong in the schools. If we all were Roman Catholics, we might agree that techniques of contraception should not be included in such courses, and that abortion is a sin. If we all were fundamentalists, we might agree that the Old Testament version of creation precludes the teaching of evolution. But we are not alike. What, then, shall be taught?

In a society with a single religion or a nation with an official church, religious instruction is accepted as an essential part of education. Religious belief is integrated into all subjects of instruction, prayer is a part of the school's routine, religious holidays are observed, and books that might create doubts about one's faith are censored. Often the teachers are members of religious orders.

But in a diverse society such as the United States, or the Rome of Epictetus's time, any effort to include religion in the curriculum of the public schools immediately raises the question, "Whose religion?" The Founding Fathers, because they could not agree on the answer to that question, and because they wanted freedom for all, set up a barrier between church and state with the establishment clause of the First Amendment to the U.S. Constitution, which reads: "Congress shall make no law respecting an establishment of religion, or prohibiting the free exercise thereof." Because public schools are instruments of the state, courts have ruled that this makes the teaching of religion unconstitutional.

The constitutional barrier was often ignored by schools located in communities where all, or nearly all, the families were Christians. Throughout the nineteenth and the first half of the twentieth centuries, recitation of the Lord's Prayer was common practice; some teachers read verses from the Bible at the beginning of the school day; and Christian holidays were observed while the holidays of Jews and other minorities were ignored. But when such practices were challenged, the courts ruled them unconstitutional.

Today, efforts are being made to amend the Constitution to permit prayer in public schools. This again raises the questions, "Whose religion? What prayers?" These questions are essential because the children in a typical school are of many faiths.

According to figures compiled by the National Council of Churches, only 49.7% of all Americans are members of *any* church. But there is great variation in different parts of the country. In predominantly Catholic Rhode Island, and mostly Mormon Utah, 75% of the people are church members, but in Washington, Oregon, California, Nevada, Hawaii, and Alaska the percentage ranges from 36% down to 29%.[1]

The U.S. Census for 1980 gives somewhat higher figures for church members, probably because it counts as members all those who, when asked, "What is your religion?" say Protestant, Catholic, or Jewish, even though they are not members of and never attend a church. The bureau reports that about 50 million Americans are Roman Catholics; 4 million are members of various Eastern Catholic denominations; 6 million are Jews; and 73 million are Protestants, divided among 35 or 40 denominations that include Unitarians, Episcopalians, Congregationalists, Presbyterians, Lutherans, Methodists, Baptists, Pentecostals, Seventh-day Adventists, Latter-day Saints, Christian Scientists, Mennonites, Jehovah's Witnesses and many others. There are also 60,000 Buddhists, as well as some native Americans who adhere to tribal faiths. The Census Bureau does not report the number of Muslims, but other sources estimate the number as high as a quarter of a million.[2]

Depending on which figures we accept, the number of Americans who are not members of any church is somewhere between 80 million and 115 million. This is the real majority or at least a plurality. It includes Deists, agnostics, and atheists, plus a very large number who are simply indifferent to religion and prefer not to be affiliated with any church. Consequently, it is inaccurate to refer to the United States as a "Christian nation" unless an adjective such as "predominantly" is inserted. Even though the majority of our ancestors were of the Christian-Judaic tradition, in religion, as in other respects, ours is a pluralistic nation. This is what most Americans want it to be.

School Prayer

The right of individual children to pray during school hours has never been denied. Children may utter silent prayers of their own choosing while the teacher is talking, while other students are reciting, or during a study hour. Many have done just that, especially around examination time.

The controversy concerns the desirability and constitutionality of permitting a teacher to ask all children to pray aloud together, or face the embarrassment of not praying while others are.

Is it possible to write a prayer acceptable to everyone? Some 25 years ago the New York State Board of Regents tried and came up with a text that they thought might satisfy most Catholics, Protestants, and Jews: "Almighty God, we acknowledge our dependence on Thee, and we beg Thy blessings on us, our parents, and our country."

The school board of Hyde Park ordered that this prayer be said aloud by each class in the presence of a teacher at the beginning of each school day. The order was challenged and the issue was taken to court. The New York Court of Appeals, with two judges dissenting, upheld the order. But in 1962 the U.S. Supreme Court overruled the decision, saying in part:

> We think that by using its public school system to encourage recitation of the Regent's prayer, the State of New York has adopted a practice wholly inconsistent with the Establishment Clause. . . . It is neither sacrilegious nor antireligious to say that each separate government in this country should stay out of the business of writing or sanctioning official prayers and leave that purely religious function to the people themselves and to those the people chose to look to for religious guidance.[3]

The Court also said that the purpose of its decision was to guard religious practice against the kind of political restraints European governments had imposed over the centuries.

Prior to this 1962 decision, the state laws concerning religion in the schools were a bundle of ambiguities. Bible reading was *required* by statute in 11 states, permitted by statute in five others, and had been upheld by courts without benefit of statute in seven others, but was specifically prohibited by the constitution of one state and had been found unconstitutional by state courts in six states. In at least six other states the language of the law and opinions of the attorney general suggested that Bible reading might be considered unconstitutional. Also in 1962, recital of the Lord's Prayer was permitted by statute in four states and had been permitted by court rulings in seven others. Two states, by statute, permitted recital of the Ten Commandments.[4]

The Supreme Court's decision seemed to put an end to the confusion, but the protest was immediate and vehement. Cardinal Spellman of New York, in a speech printed in the *Congressional Digest*, deplored the decision, saying, "Theirs is a crusade, not for freedom of religion but for freedom *from* religion. Their goal is to strip America of all her religious traditions . . . this is the establishment of a new religion of secularism."

During the ensuing years most public schools accepted the Court's decision, although a few ignored it and continued with daily prayers. Some substituted a moment of silent prayer or meditation during which children could pray to their own God in their own way. Even this raised problems for some children. Muslims wishing to pray in their own way would find it necessary to turn toward Mecca and prostrate themselves — they might need a map and a compass.

But over the years the many citizens who felt a need for school prayers became more vocal and more willing to endorse a constitutional change. By the late Seventies this had become a political issue. In 1982 President Reagan proposed an amendment to the Constitution that would permit "individual or group prayer in public schools." The wording is puzzling in view of the fact that individual prayer has never been prohibited, but the intent is clear.

Leaders of the Moral Majority enthusiastically approved, but other religious leaders were critical of the President's proposal. Dr. James Dunn, executive director of the Baptist Joint Committee on Public Affairs, said:

> Real prayer — prayer that comes from the heart — is free and personal. No government permit is needed. As Justice Stevens said, "organized prayer amounts to compelled ritual." President Reagan's proposal would guarantee strife; mock the meaning of prayer; violate the consciences of children; misuse the public schools; and rob home, churches and synagogues of their sacred tasks. I oppose state-approved, watered-down, anything-goes school prayer because I believe in genuine prayer.[5]

The Rev. Charles V. Bergstrom, executive director, Office for Governmental Affairs of the Lutheran Council in the U.S.A., said in an interview:

> As an evangelical Christian, I believe that mandated prayer can distort what prayer really is — a personal communion with God. It is a religious experience and therefore belongs in the home or church. . . . Also involved are social-justice issues. Every child has a right to go to public school without any pressure on his or her religious faith or, if he or she has no faith, any effort to bring religion into that experience, or make this a Christian nation.[6]

The Rev. M. William Howard, past president of the National Council of Churches and former executive director of the Black Council of the Reformed Church of America, says:

Advocates of public school prayer have presented this matter as a contest between believers and atheists, but I predict that any such conflict will not be nearly
as disruptive as the conflict that will surface between believers and other
believers. . . .

The surest way for us to guarantee our precious freedom of religion is to keep
the government out of the business of religious devotion. There are already many
positive options open to us to keep alive our valued religious customs without
getting the government or government-related institutions involved.

The first thing we need to do as parents is to take more responsibility for the
religious training of our children. The very best places for religious guidance are
the home and the house of worship.[7]

But the Southern Baptists endorsed Reagan's proposal; Roman Catholics
voiced support through their national administrative board; the Greek Orthodox Church backed the proposal, as did various conservative evangelical
groups. This adds up to a formidable coalition.

Both Gallup and Harris polls found that a majority of Americans support
the proposal. But, in a *constitutional* democracy the majority does not always
prevail on the basis of a poll taken at any given moment. Ours is a government
of majority rule, but minority rights. It seems entirely possible that there are
times when the majority might vote against freedom of speech, freedom of the
press, or freedom of the individual to refuse to testify against himself in a
criminal trial. The Bill of Rights was designed to protect individuals from majority opinion in times of stress.

Speaking to a convention of the Knights of Columbus on 3 August 1982,
President Reagan said, "I think you'll agree with me. We need a prayer
amendment, we need it badly," and, echoing the words of Cardinal Spellman,
he added, "We are to have freedom *of* religion, not freedom *from* religion."

Perhaps that audience did agree, but a great many Americans who are
familiar with the long history of persecution of those considered "heretics" or
"infidels" will not agree. They interpret religious freedom to mean not merely
the right to choose among established churches, but freedom to reject all
religious belief. Up to now they have had the protection of the Constitution
and the courts. If the proposed amendment becomes the law of the land we
shall have moved a long way toward the denial of that freedom.

Evolution

*The ranger said the river dug the canyon, Mommy, but you said God
did it. Who's right?*

(Caption for a cartoon in "Family Circus")

The little boy looking down into the Grand Canyon was asking a question
that has troubled cosmologists and theologians for centuries — one that takes
us deep into the basic problem of epistemology: In our search for knowledge
and for truth, shall we draw our conclusions from empirical evidence and ra-

tional thought or shall we rely on faith, revelation, religious authority, and divinely inspired books?

The problem goes far beyond the controversy over evolution of species. It includes the question of whether the earth, the solar system, and the galaxies came into existence by divine fiat only a few thousand years ago or have evolved through natural processes over billions of years, and the question of whether there was a guiding spirit to provide the design of the cosmos. The answer determines the way we teach astronomy, geology, archeology, anthropology, biology, and the origin of the human race.

Astronomers and geologists have accumulated evidence that the earth, the solar system, and the universe or cosmos have been here for a very long time. Their present estimate is that the "Big Bang" occurred some 15 billion years ago and that the solar system came into existence about 4 billion years ago. Astronomers cite evidence that the light now reaching us from distant stars has been traveling for millions of years; that what we now see is not what *is* there but what *was* there. Geologists and biologists interpret the fossils, and their location in sedimentary rocks, as evidence of forms of life billions of years ago.

Since ancient times some scientists and writers such as Lucretius have been at least vaguely aware of evolutionary processes. And since the publication of Darwin's *Origin of Species* in 1859, most scientists have come to accept the view that plants and animals have evolved slowly over millions of years and that the human species evolved similarly.

At first many theologians rejected this interpretation, particularly the part of it that concerns the origin of man; but in time most theologians of the major Christian and Jewish denominations came to terms with it, concluding that there is no fundamental conflict between their religious views and the discoveries of science. Indeed, many of the scientists have been members of religious orders. Most theologians now accept the view that the Old Testament version of creation is allegorical or that the first six days as described in Genesis can be interpreted to mean six eons or periods rather than six earthly days of 24 hours each. But there have remained a substantial number of fundamentalists who insist on a literal interpretation of Genesis and fear that the science taught in schools will undermine religious faith. In many communities science teachers have come into conflict with such groups.

The never-ending battle for academic freedom to teach a subject as it is interpreted by leading scholars in the field is waged at all academic levels. But public school teachers who engage in the battle run a far greater risk, and hence need greater courage, than do teachers in a university. Professors who defend the right of their students to learn the truth, as scientists view it, know they can count on the support of their colleagues and of the academic community. But public school teachers who demand the same freedom for their students cannot be assured of such support. For them it is often a lonely battle, subject to the prejudices of community members who are unable to grasp the significance of the issues at stake. In this respect, the experience of John Scopes was an exception.

In 1925 the nation's newspapers gave headline attention to the trial in Tennessee of John Scopes, a young high school teacher who admitted having taught the principles of evolution despite a state law prohibiting it. Scopes had volunteered to be the defendant in a test case of the law.

The trial itself was a gaudy carnival, which H. L. Mencken dubbed "The Monkey Trial." William Jennings Bryan rushed to Tennessee to aid the prosecution; Clarence Darrow assisted the defense. Scopes was convicted, and the American Civil Liberties Union paid his $100 fine. Soon thereafter he was given a scholarship to pursue his graduate studies at the University of Chicago. He became a successful oil geologist, but he was lost to the teaching profession.

Although the Tennessee law remained on the books, the publicity surrounding the trial and Darrow's success in making Bryan's views seem ridiculous to educated people made it easier for teachers in most parts of the nation to present scientific interpretations of the evidence for evolution without fear of reprisal. But Scopes said later, "The mere presence of such a law is a club over the heads of the timid. Legislation that tampers with academic freedom is not protecting society as its authors piously proclaim. By limiting freedom they are making robot factories out of schools."[8]

Fundamentalists remained unconvinced. In the 1970s, with the energetic support and growing political clout of the Moral Majority, they succeeded in getting state legislators to agree that their view of creation should be taught in the schools.

The new Creationists are more sophisticated than those of Bryan's day. They couch their theory of creation in more plausible terms and present it as a new science. They do not insist that the study of evolution be eliminated from the schools, only that equal time be given to Creationists' views. As a result, laws have been passed in a few states requiring teachers to present evolution as "just a theory" and to present Creationism as an equally valid theory. Courts have recently overturned such laws in both Arkansas and Louisiana, but the controversy keeps popping up in different communities and makes teachers uneasy about what they can teach and how they should teach it.

The controversy is further confused by the fact that people use the word *theory* in different ways. To many people it means little more than a hypothesis, a conjecture, or a guess. But the origin of the universe and of life that is taught by scientists is much more than "just a theory" in this sense. It is, rather, a complex set of principles based upon an enormous amount of evidence and on rational interpretation of the evidence.

In January 1982 the Board of Directors of the American Association for the Advancement of Science denounced any "forced teaching of creationists' beliefs in public schools" and added, "Creationists groups are imposing their beliefs disguised as science upon teachers and students to the detriment and distortion of public education in the United States . . . creationist 'science' has no scientific validity and should not be taught as science in the schools because the vast majority of scientists, who support the theory of evolution, believe scientific evidence shows that life began several million years ago and the earth is billions of years old."[9]

The great majority of scientists, as well as the majority of educated people, agree with this view. But the underlying epistemological problem remains unresolved. I once taught a class in philosophy in which most of the students accepted the scientific evidence, but one young man, who was already a minister in a fundamentalist church, rejected it in favor of a literal interpretation of Genesis. When the others challenged him by asking, "But how can you explain the fossils?" his reply was unequivocal. "If God could create the world in six days — as he could and did — it would have been a simple matter for him to toss in a few fossils to test the faith of skeptics." The others found it difficult to come up with a satisfactory rebuttal.

And there it stands today, faith vs. evidence.

Humanistic Values

Much of Christian polemic, full of that theologian's cuss word "secularism" overstates its case. The overwhelming majority of Christians in America do not believe . . . that "secularism" is a bad thing. Most Americans, religious or not, want secular politics without any churchly parties; they want secular schools, not committed to any doctrine under religious control.[10]

William Lee Miller

As a matter of fact, true religion and true humanism are not so far apart as people often assert. . . . The answers may be different but the goal is the same. Both intend to lead man beyond a materialistic and instinctive existence toward ever transcendent conceptions of the self.[11]

Robert Ulich

The Reverend Jerry Falwell, in his campaign to convert all Americans to his own brand of fundamentalism, has chosen "secular humanism," or sometimes "Godless humanism," as his favorite target. In a full-page advertisement, published 25 March 1981, he said, "We strongly oppose the teaching of the religion of secularism in public school classrooms." He has repeatedly said the same thing in televised broadcasts. This must come as a surprise to many of his followers who probably never heard of Godless humanism, secular humanism, or any other kind of humanism until he brought it up. Teachers were equally surprised to learn that they had been teaching "the religion of secular humanism."

Humanism, of course, is not a religion, though it can be incorporated into religious beliefs. The medieval humanists such as Petrarch, Erasmus, and Thomas More were among the Christian scholars of the Renaissance — many of them members of religious orders — who stressed human values at a time when other theologians concerned themselves only with God's values. They also urged a revival of classical learning as opposed to strictly ecclesiastical studies. The Encyclopaedia Britannica says, "Though humanism gradually became identified with studies of the classics, it more properly embraces any attitude exalting man's relationship to God, his free will, and his superiority over nature. Philosophically, humanism made man the measure of all things."

The word *humanities* is derived from the Latin *humanitas* which means "humanity" or "humaneness" and was introduced into the school curriculum by Italian humanists of the Renaissance. Today a major segment of the curriculum of every liberal arts college and university graduate school, public or private, consists of the humanities — the disciplines that teach human values and the spirit of man. Consequently, an assault on humanism carries with it a threat to higher education, both public and private, as well as to the public schools.

Some of the leaders of higher institutions are aware of the threat. In 1981 President Giamatti of Yale wrote a letter to the freshman class of his university saying, in part, "A self-proclaimed Moral Majority and its satellite or client groups, cunning in the use of a native blend of old intimidation and new technology, threaten the values of [liberal education]."

Although medieval humanists were criticized by orthodox theologians, and some came under the scrutiny of the Inquisition, most of them remained within the church and considered themselves Christians. Today's humanists are more diverse. Some are Jewish, some are Roman Catholics, and some are Protestants. Karl Barth, who died in 1968, was an ecumenical Christian theologian who emphasized the uniqueness of man as a being created in the image of God. Other present-day humanists hold to value systems that do not include a belief in God. It is these, presumably, that the Moral Majority have in mind when they speak of "Godless humanism." But all humanists believe in human freedom, human dignity, humane values, and the importance of working for the welfare of all mankind. Many are distinguished scholars, scientists, artists, musicians, and writers. Some are statesmen. Others are less famous but liberally educated men and women whose views cannot be ignored or lightly brushed aside. And many of the children of these humanists, including those who do not believe in any religion, are pupils in the public schools.

What the leaders of the Moral Majority fail to understand, or are unwilling to concede, is that all Americans have a right to embrace humanistic values if we choose to do so just as we have a right to choose among religions. We may choose religious humanism, secular humanism, or Godless humanism. That right is a part of our tradition and our heritage. It is guaranteed by the Constitution.

Let us hope that our legislators and our President, in their eagerness to win the votes of the Moral Majority, do not persist in their attempts to remove that right by weakening the barrier between church and state. If they do, many of our best teachers, scholars, artists, writers, and scientists will find it necessary to migrate to a freer land. We cannot afford to lose them.

Sex Education

For as long as I can remember — and my memory for such things goes back into the Twenties — we have been hearing about something called a "sexual revolution." Students of the flapper era, who liked to identify themselves with the "lost generation," dated the revolt from World War I. Students of the Thirties believed it began with the Depression, which made early marriage impossible for many who consequently looked for other sexual outlets. Those of the Fifties thought the revolution was an aftermath of World War II and began when returning veterans encountered "patriotic" coeds. Today's students think the revolution started just a few years ago, when they were in grade school, and is somehow related to both the threat of nuclear war and the invention of the Pill; though how they conclude that the Pill has made it safe and legitimate to engage in sex when most of them don't use it — or any other effective contraceptive — escapes me.[12]

All these views reflect the innocence of youth, for neither sexual activity nor the open discussion of it is as new as they believe. In 1721 Harvard undergraduates formally debated the question, "Whether it be fornication to lye with one's sweetheart before marriage." History does not record the outcome of this forensic encounter — it may have been a draw — but after 260 years the topic still is debated, not only at Harvard but by students in junior high school.

It is unlikely that there has ever been a generation to whom sex was not a major interest or which did not include many individuals who violated the rules laid down by their elders. It requires no great knowledge of history to know that the sexual mores are no more relaxed today than they have been in many times long past, and that the loosening and tightening of the restrictions on sexual activity goes in cycles of irregular length, which are related to a wide variety of social forces and social changes. There is no doubt, however, that sexual activity among high school students is more frequent today than it has been at any previous time in the memory of those now living.

The current trend toward a loosening of restraints dates roughly from the 1890s. It is not so much a revolution as a growing reaction against the restrictions that have been variously, and somewhat carelessly, described as "Puritanical," "Victorian," or "Middle-Class." The trend was accelerated by the invention of the automobile, improvements in techniques of birth control, wars that took young men away from the restraining influences of home environments, and the dislocation of families resulting from the move from farms and small towns to larger cities. Freer sexual activity was made to seem more necessary by the careless reading of Freud, and more normal — at least statistically — by the careful reading of Alfred Kinsey. It gave rise to and fed upon the literature, motion pictures, and television programs of the twentieth century. And it is encouraged by the present practice of labeling pornographic pictures, "For mature audiences only." Every adolescent wants to be mature.

Whatever the changes in frequency and kinds of activity — and we have no reliable statistics for earlier generations — there has been a vast change in the advice given to young people. A half century ago the books of intimate advice for boys and girls told readers that any sexual activity outside of marriage was sinful, and that premarital sex precluded the possibility of a happy marriage because no man respected a girl who allowed what were then called "liberties." Even then, many girls knew better, but that is what they were told.

Some of the books read by teenagers today still advise against premarital intercourse, but the reasons given are practical and psychological rather than ethical. Many of the authors say that a modest amount of petting and fondling is a normal way of showing affection and that such preliminary activities are a necessary prelude to good marital adjustment. And every teenager has read at least one book by a psychiatrist, psychologist, or possibly a minister, who sagely pontificates that, while caution is advisable and love is important, no activity involving two consenting adults is necessarily harmful or really sinful. Many adolescents are certain that they are adults and that the consent can be obtained, if necessary with the aid of the book that can be discussed on the next date.

The dilemma faced by adolescents is clear enough. Males reach their period of greatest sexual vigor and desire at an age when the doors to socially approved sexual activity are closed to them. But these doors, which have never been successfully locked and barred, have now been opened wide by a more permissive society. The dilemma faced by girls is no less perplexing. Though some adolescent girls have strong sexual urges, more are motivated by desire to be popular with boys or to please one particular boy. In the absence of an effective and accepted code, each boy or girl must decide where to draw the line. This places an enormous strain on each individual, for, as Richard Hettlinger reminds us, "There is no field of human activity in which it is so easy to deceive oneself and to be convinced by arguments which are in fact nothing but rationalizations of claimant desires."[13]

Anyone aware of the current incidence of teenage pregnancy and venereal disease must admit that young people need more accurate information about sex and its consequences. Increased activity has not been accompanied by better understanding. But, in a diverse and fluid society, in which the mores are changing rapidly, it is scarcely to be wondered that anything called *sex education* can quickly become a focus of controversy, for it is impossible to discuss the subject without proposing, or at least implying, some sense of values. If a teacher avoids all value judgments, students are likely to conclude that one choice is as good as another. A neutral stand is, in itself, a value judgment — a judgment that it is best not to decide. But young people must make some decisions.

When I was education editor at *Saturday Review* we received many letters asking why we rarely dealt with sex. Some asked if we were afraid of the subject, and one writer darkly hinted that it must be one of our taboos. The truth was that our editors had no fear of sex, either the word or the activity, and, so far as I was aware, *Saturday Review*, when under the editorship of Norman Cousins, had no editorial taboos. We knew that sex has been both a problem and a joy to the human race ever since Eve tempted Adam with the apple, and we favored increasing the joy by solving the problems.

But we found *sex education* an elusive term. To some it seemed to mean only the biology of reproduction — where babies come from and why. But a student could learn all about reproduction without gaining an understanding of sex. In any case, reproduction is a topic to be included in a course in biology and cannot really be called *sex education*.

To others it seemed to mean, "How do I behave on a date?" or "How far shall I go before marriage?" — the sort of things discussed by Ann Landers, who is much more willing to make firm pronouncements than any teacher is likely to be. This subject is of perennial concern to boys and girls because both their natural proclivities and the accepted pattern of behavior within the peer group differ greatly from the mores handed down to us. Adolescents are torn by conflict between their urges and their superegos. Many need help in handling the conflict.

To still others, sex education means instruction in the various behavior patterns involved in sexual encounters, in the subtle and complex emotional problems related to sex, and in such things as homosexuality, rape, group sex, birth control techniques, and abortion.

But the question of who is best qualified to instruct youth on such problems is a perplexing one. Many parents are unsuccessful because of the barrier between the generations. Ministers do their best but reach only a minority even of those in their own congregations, and some have neither the experience nor the information necessary. Physicians understand reproduction and disease, but most have no special preparation for discussing either psychological or moral issues.

This leaves the teachers. What can they do to instruct students on matters of sex? Although some have little more maturity or knowledge of sex than their students, others who do have the maturity, knowledge, and wisdom might do quite a lot. But which teachers, and how should they be prepared for the task? And what should they teach that is not taught in other courses? Biologists already instruct students in the biology of reproduction except in those communities where self-appointed custodians of an earlier morality insist on keeping children in ignorance. Teachers of literature who discuss problems of love and sex rarely encounter difficulty as long as they talk about characters who lived far away and long ago. But it is questionable whether the study of the loves of Romeo and Juliet or of Anthony and Cleopatra is of much help to students in solving their own problems. Social studies teachers are aware of the social and psychological problems but are even more unwilling than the others to come to any firm conclusions. And the students want some answers.

After pondering these problems, I wrote an editorial for the 18 December 1965 issue of *Saturday Review*. The massive response gave evidence that most of our readers, including leaders of several religious denominations — Congregationalists, Presbyterians, and Methodists — saw a need for more and better sex education. Gallup polls give evidence that a majority of parents agree. In 1970, when asked, "Do you approve or disapprove of schools giving courses in sex education?" 72% of public school parents said "approve."[14]

This evidence of public approval makes it apparent that sex education is here to stay. But teachers who accept responsibility for teaching such a course should know what they are getting into. They will quickly find themselves discussing problems on which the courts, legislatures, scientists, and theologians have been unable to agree. Questions will be asked about abortion whether or not the topic is included in the textbook or syllabus. The underlying question is whether a fetus is a separate human being, entitled to all the rights guaranteed by the U.S. Constitution, or still a part of the mother's body with which she is free to deal as she wishes. When does it become a separate human individual? — at conception, at quickening, at the seventh month, whenever it would be possible for it to live outside the mother's body, or not until the moment of actual birth?

A bill introduced by Senator Jesse Helms of North Carolina, declares that human life begins at conception. If it should become the law of the land, it could be interpreted to mean that anyone responsible for an abortion is guilty of murder or at least manslaughter. This, presumably, is what the sponsors of the bill intend it to mean; and a substantial minority of Americans, including leaders of some churches, support such a view.

At the other extreme are those who want abortion on demand, regardless of the reason for it, and contend that a woman has a right to do what she pleases with her own body and that a fetus is part of her body until the baby is born. This is a philosophical or theological question, not one to which a physician, scientist, or teacher can give an authoritative answer. But it is one of concern to adolescents. A teacher who says, "It is up to each individual to decide for himself or herself," is not being helpful to the frightened pregnant girl who happens to be in the class.

The subject of homosexuality will come up; it cannot be avoided. Some students need information because of their own propensities, others because of pressures from associates. But how best to present it is complicated by the fact that psychologists, psychiatrists, and biologists still disagree as to whether homosexual tendencies result from inherited characteristics or from early conditioning. Furthermore, theologians, parents, and many other people still disagree as to whether homosexual activities are sinful or just another lifestyle.

If statistical evidence, such as that from the Kinsey reports and other more recent studies, is introduced, and students learn that 30% or 60% of young people of their own age are engaging in this or that form of sexual behavior, they are likely to conclude that it must be acceptable if so many are indulging. Those who have resisted their impulses could very well feel left behind.

Teachers of courses in sex education need tact and common sense, maturity, good judgment, plus a great deal of accurate information and a considerable amount of wisdom. It is not a job for those who are merely enthusiastic about the new sexual freedom and eager to promote their own convictions.

Some things definitely should be taught without hedging. Every adolescent, male or female, should learn that anyone who engages in the activities that produce a child must accept long-term responsibility for the nurture and welfare of that child, whether or not the pregnancy was intended. He or she should learn that the institution of marriage was developed, in part, to assure such responsibility, and that avoiding marriage does not entitle parents to evade their duty to the child. A boy must learn that the fact that a girl has a reputation for being promiscuous or "easy" does not relieve him of responsibility for the child he fathers.

Students should be made aware of the risks involved in each of the many methods of birth control. They should be aware of the dangers of venereal disease, including the current epidemic of venereal herpes. Young people should also become aware of the need for mutual respect, trust, and love between sexual partners, and of the advantages that a continuing, responsible relationship has compared to trivial passing encounters.

Some teachers do an admirable job with these courses despite the difficulties. Elizabeth Mooney, author of Phi Delta Kappa fastback #47, *The School's Responsibility for Sex Education*, sounds like such a teacher. She says, "Today we are not training students in our schools of education with these qualifications. We are not even coming close. We are not encouraging students in anthropology and psychology who have had a good background in biology to get the other qualifications so desperately needed to provide a good background as a sex educator." Unfortunately, she does not tell us in this fastback how she deals with problems such as homosexuality and abortion.

Character Education

Education has as its object the formation of character.
                                                            Herbert Spencer

Knowledge without integrity is dangerous and dreadful.
                                                            Samuel Johnson

The very spring and root of honesty and virtue lie in good education.
                                                            Plutarch

It is virtue . . . which is the hard and valuable part to be aimed at in education.

John Locke

Although many writers stress the importance of character, few seem willing to define it; even lexicographers are prone to talk around the subject instead of offering clear-cut definitions. It appears, however, that most people use the word when referring to those relatively persistent or stable personality traits that have moral or ethical implications. Like other personality traits, it presumably develops as a result of all of a child's experiences — interactions with teachers, parents, religious leaders, and peer group, as well as everything heard, seen, or read, plus, quite possibly, some unidentified genetic components.

Character is more easily illustrated than defined. George Washington is often called our greatest president. He was not the best educated, it is doubtful that he was the most intelligent, and he seems to have been more admirable than likeable; but it is widely agreed that he had the traits of character needed to win the Revolutionary War and to set the new nation on its path to greatness. When others wavered, he was resolute; when others panicked, he remained calm; when others were willing to give up, he pressed on; and he made sound decisions under stress. He had a large measure of courage, integrity, fortitude, dignity, assurance, and command presence. These are traits of character.

There are others. Edward A. Wynne, editor of *Character Policy*, says:

> When we think about the connotations of *character*, we think of people who told the truth under temptation, made and kept commitments, were generous, were kind, and otherwise demonstrated what we think of as the Boy Scout (or Girl Scout) virtues. Mental discipline is surely fine, but character is first an emotional discipline — the ability to control our emotions so that they do not lead us to act against higher obligations.[15]

Although responsibility for character development is shared with others, educators cannot escape their own responsibility. It is an awesome task, made more awesome by the fact that we are uncertain just how to go about it.

It seems reasonable to assume that the books read by children affect character development in one way or another. Parson Weems, who concocted the fable about Washington and the cherry tree, thought he could build character by telling children tales (however false) about the outstanding truthfulness, honesty, and virtue of children who later became famous men or women. This may have some effect on some naive young children, but others are skeptical of moral tales even at an early age. As a boy I read the books by Horatio Alger; they provided an evening's entertainment and were more interesting than homework. But even as a 12-year-old I noted that while Alger's hero always was honest, hard-working, truthful, and virtuous, he also found it advantageous to marry the boss's daughter. Of course he fell in love with her first, but since she was charming, that was easy.

Because serious literature delves more deeply into problems of character, it probably has more lasting effect on the reader, but the cause-and-effect relationship is not easily demonstrated.

Wellington denied having said that the battle of Waterloo was won on the playing fields of Eton, but the fact that so many people quoted the remark, and attributed it to him, indicates that many believe that competitive sports build character. It is true that an athlete learns to work as a member of a team and to press on even when greatly fatigued. But I have observed that when a coach says, "We are building character this year," he means that his team has been losing. Clearly, he would prefer to win.

It is difficult to see how the school can counteract the influence of television on children who spend more hours before the tube than in the classroom. From television children learn that it is permissible not only for the good guy to kill the bad guy — without a trial or any legal procedure — but also to decide for himself who the bad guy is. Though television producers insist that there is "no positive proof" that their shows encourage crime, we know that children learn from all their experiences, and watching bloody mayhem in living color is surely an experience. While we wait for more positive proof, it seems reasonable to assume that television must have some influence on the character of children, and that the influence is frequently bad.

Public schools have been criticized for failing to develop good character, and it is true that they have not been notably successful. Do nonpublic schools do any better? I do not know the answer and doubt that anyone does. Private schools, in brochures boasting about their programs, emphasize that they "build character," although they cite no evidence. Those who run boarding schools ought to do better because they have custody of the child for 24 hours a day. But the parents of such children have much less opportunity to build character than do parents whose children spend some part of the evening and weekend at home.

Researchers wishing to investigate the relative influence on character of public, private, and parochial schools (there ought to be material here for a good doctoral dissertation) might begin by seeking answers to questions such as these: What percentage of the congressmen convicted of taking bribes received their education in each kind of school? What is the school background of public employees who become spies and embezzlers and of crooked stockbrokers or citizens who cheat on their income taxes? How many of the members of the Mafia or of Al Capone's gang were products of parochial schools?

Many other variables, involving many intercorrelations, would have to be taken into account before conclusions could be reached, but even the answers to these simple questions might be revealing. We might discover that years spent in even the best private or parochial schools give no assurance of high moral character, however devoted to that goal the teachers may be. Quite possibly, all schools are failing in this regard and no one knows just what to do about it.

It seems probable that a school's best contribution to character development is made, not by special courses or specific acts, but as an indirect result of all that we do and of our own character as it is perceived by our students. Clear rules of behavior, fairly enforced, may help; but I doubt that character is greatly influenced by school prayer, ritualized pledges of allegiance, or the close-order drill of which military schools think so highly. Character is a by-product — a very important by-product — of a good school and good teachers, whether the school is public, private, or parochial.

---

1. *U.S. News & World Report,* 11 October 1982, p. 13.
2. *Statistical Abstract of the U.S.,* 1981, pp. 52-53.
3. Engel v. Vitale, 370 U.S. 421, 82 S. Ct. 1261 (1962).
4. Adapted from the July 1962 issue of *School Life,* a U.S. Office of Education Publication. *See also Saturday Review,* 17 November 1962.
5. *Family Weekly,* 4 July 1982.
6. *U.S. News & World Report,* 15 November 1982, p. 73.
7. "Whose Prayer?" *Education Week,* 1 September 1982, p. 24.
8. John Scopes, *Center of the Storm* (New York: Holt, Rinehart & Winston, 1968).
9. *Chronicle of Higher Education,* 13 January 1982.
10. William Lee Miller, "The Fight Over America's Fourth 'r,' " *Great Issues in Education* (Chicago: Great Books Foundation, 1956), p. 27.
11. Robert Ulich, *Philosophy of Education* (New York: American Book Co., 1961), p. 114.
12. Segments of this section have been adapted from my editorials and articles in *Saturday Review.*
13. Richard Hettlinger, *Living with Sex, The Student's Dilemma* (New York: The Seabury Press, 1966).
14. Stanley Elam, ed., *A Decade of Gallup Polls of Attitudes Toward Education, 1969-1978* (Bloomington, Ind.: Phi Delta Kappa, 1978).
15. Edward A. Wynne, "Rigorous Thinking About Character," *Phi Delta Kappan* 64 (November 1982):187.

4

How Shall We Deal with Individual Differences?

Amongst men of equal education there is great inequality of abilities . . . the woods of America as well as the schools of Athens produce men of several abilities. [1]

John Locke

Locke was well aware of the influence of both heredity and environment in producing ability of all kinds. His comments above, and elsewhere in his writings, suggest that he was uncertain of which is the stronger.

After 300 years and vast quantities of research, we are still uncertain. Some psychologists who have examined the evidence conclude that from 60% to 80% of the measured differences in intellectual capacity results from heredity, but others familiar with the same evidence make a much smaller estimate. Some think the influence of heredity is almost negligible compared to environmental influences in early childhood.

All too often the interpreters are influenced by what they wish were true or think ought to be true. Scholars of liberal persuasion, who believe deeply in human equality, are understandably reluctant to accept any interpretation that might suggest genetic differences related to sex, race, ethnic background, or social class. Those who investigate the possibility of such differences have been accused of sexism, racism, or social class bias.

But nothing is gained by refusing to look at the evidence or by questioning the motives of those who do. When we examine the evidence from test scores we find a number of facts on which nearly all psychologists agree. The most important is that within each category of human beings we find a wide range of all kinds of talent and potentiality. There are geniuses of every race and of each sex and from all social classes, just as there are morons. If each student is judged as a unique individual, and treated as an individual rather than as a member of a category, the question of whether there are statistical differences among the means of the various categories becomes unimportant to a classroom teacher. The important question is, "What are the capacities and potentialities of this individual child?"

The decision not to concern ourselves with statistical differences among categories should not prevent us from facing the fact that there are enormous differences among *individuals* in capacity for learning. By the time a child enters school these differences are too great to be ignored or easily eliminated, regardless of whether they result in part from genetics or entirely from early environmental influences. Teachers can do nothing about a child's genetic structure; they can do a great deal to improve the child's opportunities for learning, if they know what that child's potentials are. The testing movement is an attempt to measure such potentials — an effort fraught with controversy.

Objective Tests

All tests given to human beings are designed to measure individual differences — differences in general aptitude for learning, special aptitudes, knowledge, skills, interest, or traits of personality. If there were no differences there would be no need for tests. Most of today's testing involves the use of objective instruments that began to replace subjective examinations early in this century because they were easier to score, had greater reliability, and could be administered to larger numbers of people.

But objective tests have always been a source of controversy. When they first were used as a basis for grading and promotion, many academic scholars rejected them, contending that a proper education must include a kind of examination designed to stretch the mind and give students an opportunity to demonstrate their ability to think logically and to express ideas with clarity. President Griswold of Yale reflected the view of many when he said in 1952, "There are some of us who still prefer the essay to the intellectual bingo game, scored by electricity."

Despite such protests, Americans now are tested from the cradle to the grave — when they enter school, repeatedly while in school, when they enter college, when they apply for admission to graduate or professional school, and before they are admitted to a profession or a skilled trade. They are tested when they apply for driver's licenses, when they enter the armed forces, and frequently when they apply for other jobs. When they approach the end of their working lives, they are not yet tested to determine their readiness for retirement, but that will come. It will be an improvement over the current practice of basing retirement entirely on chronological age.

Tests are used in various settings, but their widest use is in the schools. Early in this century educational psychologists demonstrated that individual differences of many kinds are distributed along the normal curve with most individuals falling near the mean but some far above or far below it.

The effort to provide for these individual differences took many forms. Some schools moved bright children up through the grades more rapidly than others. Others kept children of similar age in the same classroom while attempting to individualize instruction — a difficult task with a class of 30. Others grouped children by I.Q. or mental age. This was called "homogeneous grouping," but the term was inaccurate because the children in each class were still heterogeneous in physical and social maturity as well as in special aptitudes. Some schools provided fast, medium, and slow tracks; a few changed this to some variant of the dual-progress plan, which enables children to be on the fast track when studying subjects in which they excel but on a slower track for other subjects. A few educators defended the practice of providing separate schools for children at the upper and lower ends of the scale, but most preferred to keep them in the same building. But all agreed that it is as futile to *require* all children to master difficult school subjects as it would be to require all to run the mile in five minutes or to jump over a five-foot bar. Many would succeed but some would fail, even with the best teachers or coaches.

But the criticism of testing continued. Much of it centered on tests used to measure *intelligence*, a word so emotionally loaded that it seems unfortunate that it ever was used in connection with testing. If the terms *general aptitude* or *academic aptitude* had been substituted, there might have been less opposition.

To many people, intelligence seemed to imply something fixed and final, determined once and for all when the child is born. The test makers intended no such meaning. Many of them were convinced that genetic traits play a role in determining aptitudes for learning, but all agreed that environmental factors in early childhood alter test scores. Alfred Binet intended his intelligence test for use with Parisian children who shared a common language and cultural heritage. Henry H. Goddard, who brought the test to the United States, translated it into English, added new items, and standardized it with American children, estimated that about 60% of what the test measured reflected genetic influence but 40% resulted from early childhood opportunities for learning. None of the test makers said they were measuring inherited capacity directly or exclusively; all were aware of environmental influences.

Critics contended that intelligence cannot even be defined, much less measured. But finding a definition for intelligence is no more difficult than finding one for *time, energy,* or *gravity,* all of which appear in every dictionary. All are defined operationally.

Those who have developed tests of intelligence offer these definitions:

Intelligence is completeness of understanding, inventiveness, persistence in a given course, and critical judgment.

Alfred Binet

Intelligence is the ability to make use of past experience in meeting present problems and anticipating future problems.

Henry H. Goddard

Intelligence is the general capacity of an individual consciously to adjust his thinking to new requirements.

Wilhelm Stern

Intelligence is the ability to carry on abstract thinking.

Louis Terman

Intelligence is the ability to undertake activities that are characterized by difficulty, complexity, abstractness, economy, adaptiveness to a goal, social value, and the emergence of originals, and to maintain such activities under conditions that demand a concentration of energy and a resistance to emotional forces.

George Stoddard

These definitions are not as dissimilar as they may at first appear. All distinguish intelligence from knowledge. All agree that intelligence is a capacity or potential, not a present level of achievement.

Much of the criticism shows misunderstanding of the purposes and uses of tests. Critics charge that children from disadvantaged backgrounds are handicapped in taking tests. They surely are. But the test does not cause the disadvantage; the test merely tells us how much, and we need to know how much children are disadvantaged when we plan their school programs.

A test is a measuring instrument. If it measures what it was designed to measure, its validity is not impaired by the fact that it fails to measure other factors, traits, or qualities. A thermometer is designed to measure temperature. If it does this accurately it is a valid instrument, even though it fails to measure humidity or wind velocity and hence does not tell us whether we will be comfortable outdoors without our topcoats. Similarly, an intelligence test is valid if it measures intelligence, even though it does not measure character, personality, persistence, or motivation, and hence cannot predict which individuals will be most admirable, likeable, successful, or free of neurosis.

Like many other useful instruments, intelligence tests measure indirectly. A thermometer does not measure heat. It measures the height of a column of mercury and from this the observer infers the temperature. An intelligence test measures what an individual can do with his or her intelligence right now — how well he or she can comprehend meanings, make discriminations, draw inferences, and solve problems. From this the tester makes an inference concerning the individual's intelligence.

But some of the criticism of the way tests are used is justified. Test scores have often been misinterpreted and misused. Teachers who rely too heavily on a single group test of intelligence often expect too little from children with low scores. Some administrators have been too arbitrary in keeping children on the slow track because of low test scores, even though they are obviously doing better work than is expected of those on that track. No one who understands the difference between aptitude and achievement would interpret Scholastic Aptitude Test scores as evidence of what students have learned in school, but many people do interpret the scores that way.

Parents who learn that their child's I.Q. is in the "superior" or "very superior" range sometimes assume that the child has it made and will always achieve more than other students, overlooking the fact that millions of other children in the nation have comparable scores. Even with a high I.Q. a student still must work hard and learn a great deal before he or she can succeed in any vocation. Ten years after graduating no one will care what a person's I.Q. is. The only question will be, "What have you accomplished since graduation?"

When the Army Alpha (not really an intelligence test) was given to more than a million men during World War I and it was found that men whose ancestors were from Southern Europe scored lower, on the average, than those whose ancestors came from Northern Europe, some people jumped to the conclusion that Northern Europeans were more intelligent. A more probable explanation is that the Southern Europeans had arrived in the United States more recently, had had fewer educational opportunities, and were less familiar with American culture and the English language.

These, however, are not legitimate criticisms of the tests; they are criticisms of the way test scores have been interpreted.

The Paideia Proposal: A Denial of Individual Differences

Democracy arises out of the notion that those who are equal in any respect are equal in all respects; because men are equally free they claim to be absolutely equal.[2]

Aristotle

Over the past 30 years we have heard growing demands that the evidence from testing be ignored and that all children be offered the same education and held to the same standards. The first pronouncement of the Council for Basic Education, which began, "All children, without exception, *must . . .*" followed by a list of things they must learn, was mentioned in chapter 2. Many of those who joined in this demand were university professors of academic subjects who had become convinced that professional educators, in their eagerness to meet the needs of slow learners, had lowered standards for all students, with the result that superior students were learning less than they were capable of learning.

More recently, those who minimized the importance of individual differences were joined by social commentators who had come to believe that the American system requires not only equal *opportunity* for learning (the Jeffersonian ideal) but equal educational achievement. Some even went so far as to insist that any admission of possible genetic differences in learning capacity is un-American.

As a result of these convictions, efforts to provide for individual differences in the schools came under attack. Courts have ruled that multitrack systems are unconstitutional unless children of all races and ethnic groups are represented in each track, and that intelligence tests may no longer be used in assigning students to special classes. Some large school systems have abandoned the use of intelligence tests.

These decisions reveal confusion as to the purpose of special classes. If children need the additional assistance they will get in a special class, the fact that they are assigned to one is not discrimination against them — it is discrimination in their favor and will increase their opportunity for learning. The Binet test was originally developed to help the schools of Paris to decide which children had the greater need for special classes. If assignment is not to be made on the basis of objective tests, it will be made on the basis of subjective judgments that are less valid. Civil rights groups that take such cases to court seem to misunderstand both the purposes of testing and the reason for special classes.

But the attacks on testing continue. While the trend of the first half of the twentieth century was toward more emphasis on individual differences among children and toward greater effort on the part of educators to adapt school programs to those differences, today's trend is toward a denial of individual differences, or an insistence that the differences must be ignored by those who plan school programs.

Mortimer Adler was ahead of his time. Since the day when he was mentor to Robert Maynard Hutchins at the University of Chicago in the 1930s, he has minimized, or denied the existence of, individual differences, insisting "Men are everywhere and at all times the same." In his recently published *Paideia Proposal*[3] he says, "All children . . . have the same inherent tendencies, the same inherent powers, the inherent capacities." He softens this a bit by adding that individuals may possess these common traits in different degrees, a modification that confuses the issue because the goal of test makers has always been to measure differences in degree, not in kind. But he remains convinced that all differences have environmental origins. He says, "Preschool deprivation is the cause of backwardness and failure in school." He does not say it is *one* of the reasons — he leaves no room for possible genetic variation.

This conviction that all children have the same inherent powers and capacities leads Adler to the conclusion that all children should be enrolled in exactly the same educational program for 12 years of elementary and secondary education with no electives except for a choice among foreign languages. There must be no ability grouping, no track system — children of all levels of intelligence must be in the same class (presumably at the same chronological age) where all must meet the same standards of achievement. All must master mathematics through calculus before they leave high school. "Children who . . . manifest deficiencies that would result in their not achieving standards of performance must be given special help to overcome these deficiencies. Such help would be truly remedial — remedying deficiencies that *can and must be overcome.*" (Italics mine.)

The Paideia Program has three goals, each to be achieved through its own method of instruction: 1) The acquisition of organized knowledge by means of didactic instruction, supplemented by textbooks and other aids; 2) the development of intellectual skills of learning by means of coaching, exercises, and supervised practice; and 3) enlarged understanding of ideas and values by means of Socratic questioning plus active participation in the discussion of great books and great works of art.

The goals are admirable. They do not differ greatly from those discussed in the section on liberal education in chapter 1 of this book. The first two methods have always been used by many good teachers in all kinds of schools, although it must be admitted that teachers who use the methods effectively are all too rare. The third method is used by a few outstanding teachers in public schools, but too infrequently. If Adler can find a way of achieving these goals by teaching more teachers to use these methods effectively, he will deserve our gratitude, for no one has yet found a way. If he had proposed these goals and these methods without insisting that they will be effective with *all* the children who are enrolled in public schools, he would have made a valuable contribution. But the completely required curriculum, with the same high standards of achievement demanded of *all* children, is quite another matter. Will it work? Can it be done?

The only way to find out is to give it a fair trial with a group of children such as is found in a typical public school. Since much will depend on the teachers, and because it may be difficult to find public school teachers who have the necessary background and will accept the assignment with confidence and enthusiasm, I suggest the certification requirements be waived and that the faculty be recruited from members of the Paideia Group that has made Mortimer Adler its spokesman.

This group includes famous scholars, writers, and executives: Clifton Fadiman, Jacques Barzun, Theodore Sizer, Charles Van Doren, Ruth Love, and a number of college and university presidents. Because they believe deeply in the program, I am confident that they will be willing to devote a few years of their lives to a demonstration of its feasibility. It will be a legitimate use of their time and talents because nothing is more important than good teaching. Some financial sacrifice may be required, but they will be paid the standard teacher salaries and, because of their outstanding talents, might start at the top of the scale. Albert Shanker, whose endorsement of the *Paideia Proposal* appears on the cover of the book, should be glad to demonstrate his commitment to the improvement of educational quality by giving up his career as a union leader to join the faculty.

These teachers will accept responsibility for the education of a group of children selected to represent the *total spectrum* of human capacity for learning. The students should come from a wide range of homes, and the school should be located in a neighborhood that offers all the usual distractions. All teachers will work with the same students through all 12 grades in order that no teacher may blame a child's previous teachers for his learning deficiencies.

Mortimer Adler will join the faculty as a first-grade teacher of arithmetic and will continue to teach the same children through the twelfth grade, by which time all will be required to demonstrate proficiency with calculus, just as he proposes in his book. Except for a choice of a foreign language, the course of study will be the same for all. All will be held to the same rigorous standards.

Adler says, "Those who think the proposed course of study cannot be successfully followed by all children fail to realize that the children of whom they are thinking have never had their minds challenged by requirements such as these." Very well, we shall let Adler and his friends challenge them daily for 12 long years. Teachers will be judged by the success of their students in meeting the high standards.

If this experiment proves a success, the Paideia Group will be hailed as the saviors of public education. If any substantial number of children fail to achieve the high standards, even with these outstanding teachers, the *Paideia Proposal* will be written off as just another noble experiment, and we shall continue our search for solutions that make provision for individual differences.

How Much Education for All?

> *Prolongation of school age is in itself not a blessing, but may even be a curse to civilization unless there goes together with the prolongation a revolutionary rethinking of the total program and a restructuring of the total educational system from the secondary school upwards.*[4]
>
> Robert Ulich

When American lawmakers first decreed that schooling should be required for all children, they had no intention of providing secondary and higher education for all. Their intention was to assure widespread literacy plus sufficient knowledge of the basic disciplines to enable a self-governing nation to maintain itself. It was not until the last quarter of the nineteenth century that it occurred to educators that secondary education might be possible for all, and not until the last half of the twentieth century that some came to accept the view that higher — or at least postsecondary education — might be appropriate for all.

By 1900 the majority of the then 46 states had passed laws requiring school attendance to the age of 14; and by the 1920s half the states had raised the age to 16, though some of these allowed exceptions for those who had completed the eighth grade. Five states required attendance to the age of 16, except for those who graduated from high school earlier.

After World War II, though most of the laws were not changed, it became a part of the conventional wisdom that all boys and girls, regardless of academic interest or talent, should remain in high school until graduation. A nationwide publicity campaign called attention to the number of ''dropouts,'' even though the number had been declining steadily for a century. It was implied that dropouts were consigned to a life of unemployment, destitution, and probably crime.

Since about 1970 there has been some evidence of a reversal of public opinion. With increasing frequency, doubts have been expressed about the wisdom of requiring school attendance for adolescents who are profiting little from school and would prefer to drop out. High school teachers and principals have reported that the reluctant learners caused most of the disciplinary problems and, by their disruptive behavior in the classroom, made learning difficult for other students.

Those who still insisted that all should remain in school until the age of 18 said that compulsory attendance was necessary to ''keep them off the streets,'' overlooking the fact that schools keep boys and girls off the streets for only a few hours each day and for only half the days of the year. In any case the ''keep them off the streets'' slogan implies that the purpose of schooling is custodial rather than educational. When a school becomes a custodial institution, it loses its effectiveness as an educational institution. It becomes a prison.

Students drop out of school for a variety of reasons. Some are restless youths who cannot bear being ''cooped up,'' as they put it. Others are more seriously disturbed psychologically and need more help than can be provided by an occasional visit to a school psychologist. But some of those students who dislike school, as did many before them, will eventually be excellent workers in jobs that do not require much verbal or mathematical talent. Even in our technological, bureaucratic society, not everyone need be a technician, clerk, or bookkeeper. There still are other jobs.

Vocational courses in high school have not solved the problem. Most vocational education (as distinguished from vocational *training*, which is best provided on the job) is preparation for skilled trades or clerical work. These jobs require at least average intelligence plus willingness to work — just what many of the dropouts lack.

Some youngsters who have sufficient academic talent for high school work lack the motivation during their high school years. Adult evening classes should be provided for those who develop the motivation later, as many will.

Because motivation is essential for all school work, adolescents should go to school because they want to, or they should not go. Teachers should do all they can to enhance motivation but they cannot do it all; students also have a responsibility. Students who remain in school only because they are required to be there will feel frustrated, and frustration leads to aggression. Other students and the teachers are likely to be the targets of this aggression.

Mortimer Adler assures us that the problems of all these potential dropouts can be solved by keeping them in school, enrolling in the Paideia Program, and *requiring* them to achieve high academic standards. I wish it were that simple.

Inevitably, the question arises, "What is to become of those who leave school before they can find employment?" In an urbanized society, where the number of unskilled jobs is declining, there is no easy answer. But forced schooling is no answer unless we are willing to turn high schools into custodial institutions. Possible solutions include something like the CCC of the 1930s or other publicly supported, on-the-job training programs or, for some, the armed forces. But I would not want our nation's defenses to rely on men and women who are reluctant to learn or unable to learn. Today's armed forces require technical skills.

Society — the state or the nation — has a responsibility for those who cannot learn or refuse to learn, but the public high school cannot shoulder all of that responsibility if it is to provide good education for those who are eager to learn.

If we agree that schooling is not to be compulsory beyond early adolescence, we still face the questions: "How much should be *available* to all who want it? How much should be provided at public expense?" The burgeoning, in recent years, of community colleges with minimal entrance standards seems to suggest that state legislators — who presumably reflect the views of their constituents — are now convinced that at least two years of college should be provided for all at public expense.

Only recently has this been true. The vast expansion of American higher education has been a phenomenon of the twentieth century. In 1900 only 95,000 youngsters, or 6.2% of the age group, graduated from high school, and only 27,000 or 2% graduated from college. The annual number of college graduates rose to 48,000 in 1920, 186,000 in 1940, 400,000 in 1960, and to one million in 1980.

No other nation in history has provided higher education for so large a percentage of its youth. Today nearly 80% of our young people graduate from high school and well over half of these enter a college of some kind. Until recently even the most advanced nations of Europe assumed that if 3% to 5% of their young people became university graduates, that number would satisfy all the needs of the nation for highly educated men and women. Since World War II the percentage has been growing but it still falls far short of ours. In the U.S.S.R. one in seven high school graduates now enters some kind of advanced educational institution, but their number of high school graduates is smaller than ours.

It should be noted that comparative figures are confusing because the term "higher education" means different things in different nations. In many of the nations of continental Europe it means only graduate and professional education. Many of the subjects that our students study during their undergraduate years are taught in the German *gymnasium* or the French lycée, which are considered secondary schools.

While our colleges and universities now enroll many more students than those of other nations, our attrition rates are much higher. In England, where only 14% of the young people enter universities, 87% of these complete work for a degree. But many of our 12 million college students will never receive degrees. The fact that only about one million receive baccalaureate degrees each year tells the story.

Eric Ashby, a noted English educator who has made a careful study of American colleges, attributes our high attrition to our "liberal and diverse admissions standards." He says, "It is a part of the privilege of an affluent society to be able to sample things and reject them. But the American society may not be affluent enough to allow this privilege in higher education in the 1980s. It may then become unrealistic politically to spend millions of dollars on places in college occupied by persons who are not gifted enough, or do not have the motivation, to benefit from the education which college provides."[5]

Ashby may not have been aware that many of those who fail to receive degrees are community college students, who enroll for terminal courses or short vocational courses and have no intention of completing four-year programs. But it is true that the cost of providing space and instruction for the millions of Americans who enter college but leave without degrees is very great, running to billions of dollars annually. Faced with the present revolt against higher taxes, we must decide whether this is the best possible use of the money available for higher education.

Although some Americans now contend that colleges should be open to all, regardless of intellectual capacity, most educators agree that there is a minimal intellectual level below which any education properly called "higher" is an impossibility. Professor Fritz Machlup of Princeton, in a widely quoted statement, says, "Higher education is far too high for the average intelligence, much too high for the average interest, and vastly too high for the average patience and perseverance of the people here or anywhere." A similar conviction is reflected in the admission standards of some of the more highly selective colleges, which boast that they select their students from the upper 5% or even the upper 2% of high school graduating classes.

But so extreme a view is indefensible. Many colleges, private as well as public, have for many years admitted a much higher percentage of high school graduates. Some of the students who would have been denied admission to the prestigious colleges have made excellent records in other colleges, have gone on to graduate and professional schools, and have made significant contributions to the world as statesmen, scholars, and members of the learned professions. On the basis of their secondary school records, neither Franklin Roosevelt nor Winston Churchill could gain admission to the "most highly selective" American colleges today, nor could Einstein. Yet these individuals, and many others, profited from their college education and achieved greatly after graduation, while many of the graduates of the selective colleges remain obscure.

It does not follow, however, that higher education is appropriate for everyone. Unless the essential nature of higher education is dramatically changed, it is not appropriate for those who — even after preparatory courses — cannot read difficult books with understanding, cannot express themselves in speech or writing, or are bewildered by scientific theories and mathematical symbols. Nor is it appropriate for anyone who lacks the eagerness to learn. Higher education must always be, in some sense, selective.

The Gifted, Talented, and Creative

A universal system of education is ultimately tested at its margins. It functions fairly well in educating most students in the middle or normal range but has a tendency to be less effective with exceptional groups. . . .

The gifted and talented are a natural resource that has been largely neglected and underdeveloped . . . the intellectual atmosphere in some high schools actually creates pressure on the gifted not to achieve, but to conform and underachieve. [6]

Marsha M. Correll

The biographies of men and women who have achieved greatness include many accounts of the failure of their teachers to recognize special talents. In this respect European schools fail as completely as ours. European teachers failed to recognize the special talents of Einstein and Churchill, just as American teachers failed to recognize those of Edison.

Although most American schools make special provision for students who are physically handicapped or intellectually backwards, a much smaller number make adequate provisions for those with superior talents, either because of a belief that they can take care of themselves or an attitude that providing special attention to the gifted is elitist.

Some do survive and achieve greatness despite their schooling, but others are unable to take care of themselves. They work far below their potential level because their talents are not encouraged. Some drop out of school from sheer boredom.

The adjectives *talented* and *gifted* are applied loosely to two disparate groups. The first consists of those with talents of a high order in music, art, dance, poetry, and athletics. Of these, only the athletes receive special attention in our schools. They "make the team," get their pictures in the paper, win letters and medals; and when they are ready for college they receive athletic scholarships. A few scholarships are available for young people of outstanding musical talent, but there are very few for poets or artists.

But youngsters of exceptionally high general intelligence are also called talented or gifted, even though their talents are less specialized and their careers less predictable. These are the ones most likely to be identified by an intelligence test, for they are not always "A" students. They are the boys and girls who have keen powers of observation, who read widely without waiting for the books to be "assigned" by a teacher, who quickly develop skills in language and mathematics, who take pleasure in intellectual activity and have unusual powers of abstraction, conceptualization, and problem solving. They have an exceptional amount of intellectual curiosity, ask more questions than the adults around them can answer, and often refuse to accept the answers given. Many teachers and parents find them a problem. Only teachers or parents who are themselves of superior intelligence can fully appreciate their talents.

Various provisions are made for these students. Some schools provide a fast track; a few permit them to skip grades. Some colleges offer early admission or advanced placement; some have honors programs that offer a richer fare and greater challenge. A few large cities provide special schools, although there is growing pressure to eliminate such schools.

But many schools still keep even the most brilliant boys and girls in the classrooms with others of the same chronological age, where the work is too easy, the books too childish, the problems assigned too simple. Their intellectual curiosity goes unchallenged because the teacher is preoccupied with the problem of teaching average and below average children.

The advantages and disadvantages of special schools and special classes have been debated for decades. There is something to be said for letting bright students spend a part of their time with others of similar age but lesser talent. But children of exceptionally high intelligence should have an opportunity to spend some portion of the day, week, or year with others as bright as they and with a teacher of their own superior intellectual level.

There is no possibility of finding enough teachers with I.Q.'s of 140, 150, or higher for every classroom in the nation — even the best colleges do not succeed in that. But a child whose intelligence is of that high level — and there are some in every school system — should spend some time with a teacher who, in addition to knowing the subject and how to teach it, shares the child's acute perceptiveness, problem-solving ability, powers of conceptualization, and great intellectual curiosity.

Such teachers do exist and can be found in almost every school system, however modest the *mean* test score of public school teachers may be. More could be recruited by offering special college scholarships for bright students who want to become teachers. By means of team teaching or a dual-progress plan, it is possible to make such teachers available to the students who need them most for at least some portion of the day or week.

The concern that special education for the gifted will lead to the development of an intellectual elite is a fallacy that should be laid to rest. If there were any danger of such a possibility in America, it would come far more from private schools and colleges with high entrance standards than from special classes within a comprehensive public school.

An elite is a group of people given special privileges, recognition, and rewards. The fear that ability grouping could lead to an intellectual elite shows limited understanding of our culture. We simply are not that kind of a people. If we ever have an elite in the United States it will not be an intellectual one. In a very real sense, we already have an elite of television stars, country singers, and football players. It might not be a bad idea to try to bring the prestige, income, and recognition of our most intellectually talented people up to the same level. But the possibility that intellectuals will ever become a true elite in our country seems remote.

A third, much smaller, group is much more difficult to recognize in childhood. These are the creative geniuses — the awkward, lonely, inquiring, critical men and women — who will make the great breakthroughs in science, philosophy, literature, music, and the arts. Such creativity is difficult to recognize even in adults. Many poets, artists, and musical composers who later were to be hailed as geniuses were scorned by critics of their day and ridiculed by the people. Great scientists and philosophers have remained undiscovered until after their deaths. Inventors who have changed our lives were considered fools and dreamers by their contemporaries.

Although creative potential is positively correlated with intelligence, the two are by no means synonymous. Creativity requires something more than intelligence — some trait not clearly understood but that appears to be related to a willingness to break away from established patterns and solve problems in unconventional ways. Neither school grades nor scores on achievement tests are measures of these traits. A straight "A" student has demonstrated a willingness to work hard at an assigned task but often lacks the spirit of rebellion characteristic of the true innovator.

College entrance examiners who are impressed by students who rank high in their high school classes and have also taken part in many school activities are likely to overlook potential geniuses, who are not necessarily maladjusted but have focused their interests too sharply to be called "well-rounded" and lack the willingness to conform required of straight "A" students.

Psychologists now are working on new tests for the prediction of creativity — tests that measure "divergent thinking" rather than the correct but conventional responses. But there has not yet been time to validate these tests against the ultimate criterion — creative achievement during the adult years. My guess is that the tests will turn out to predict only the lower levels of creativity — not true genius.

Even if we learn to measure creative potential, there is some doubt about how much a school or a teacher can do to develop it. John Gardner says, "The creative process is often not responsive to conscious efforts to initiate or control it. It does not proceed methodically or in a programmatic fashion. It meanders. It is unpredictable, digressive, capricious."[7]

If a teacher ever encounters a true potential genius, perhaps the best one can do is to encourage him, teach him what one can, then step aside and let him alone. He or she differs greatly from the child who is merely intelligent.

Desegregation: Is Busing the Solution?

Racial prejudice has been a blot on our nation from the time the first slaves were brought from Africa. Until about 30 years ago, blacks were denied admission to the better hotels, restaurants, country clubs, and even many churches. In trains they rode in separate cars; in theaters they sat in the balcony; as actors in motion pictures they were allowed to play only comic or demeaning roles. No matter how skilled and talented, they were excluded from professional baseball and football teams.

Other races were also victims. When the whites arrived, native Americans were driven from their homes and onto reservations. During World War II American citizens of Japanese ancestry were interned in camps, but German- and Italian-Americans were not.

In a single generation so much progress has been made that boys and girls now in school look upon the 1950s as the Dark Ages, as indeed they were for many people. Hotels, restaurants, trains, planes, and theaters now are open to all. Numerous black athletes are on professional sports teams. Black actors and actresses now appear in significant roles in motion pictures and on television.

More needs to be done; full integration is still a long way off. But this is a problem for the adults of the nation. School children should not be asked to carry the major burden, yet that is exactly what is being asked of them. In many cities the result has been a disruption of the educational process for children of all races, because getting an education requires opportunity for thought in a calm environment without emotional turmoil. Children are not likely to learn the academic subjects while in the center of a battlefield in which parents, school officials, judges, and legislators are the warriors.

The public schools have already done their share. Except in the Deep South most public schools accepted children of all races long before the Supreme Court ruling of 1954, at a time when housing, trade unions, and professional sports still were segregated. Jesse Owens was able to become a famous athlete and holder of world records in the 1930s because he attended public schools and a state university. If he had wanted to become a professional football or basketball player he would have been denied the opportunity to compete against white athletes.

South of the Mason-Dixon Line, black children went to separate schools prior to 1954 and most of these were inferior schools despite the "separate but equal" doctrine. But since 1954 most of these have been integrated with white schools, sometimes after painful strife.

The problem of desegregation looks different to people in different kinds of communities because it *is* different. In a small town it is obvious that children of all races should attend the one school available, as they always have in most parts of the North and West, usually without much protest from anyone.

In a city with many schools, and in which people of different races live in different parts of town, the problem is more complex. Desegregation of schools while housing patterns remain segregated — either by tradition or by economic levels — requires that children be assigned to schools distant from their homes if a balance of races is to be achieved in every school.

The major metropolitan centers have additional problems, accentuated in recent years by the massive movement of middle-class families out of the inner cities and their replacement by poorer people, many of them black or Hispanic. As a result of this transfer of population, plus the growing trend of white parents in these cities to send their children to nonpublic schools, the school population of Washington, D.C., is now only 4% white, that of Detroit only 12% white, and that of Chicago 19% white. Blacks, Hispanics, and Asians outnumber whites in 33 of the 55 biggest city school systems.[8]

Establishing a balance of the races in the schools of such cities would require the transportation of children into the cities from far outside the city limits. Some courts have held that the number of children of each of the races in each school should be proportional to the number in the community.

But what is the community? For a school in Manhattan, is the community Harlem, the entire borough of Manhattan, the five boroughs, or the New York Metropolitan Area, which includes parts of Connecticut and New Jersey? If the metropolitan area is the community, establishing a balance of the races in each school would require the transportation of children for many miles, sometimes across state lines. The problem of meeting the different educational standards of all three states, and of apportioning tax revenues from three states equitably, would keep the courts tied up for years, while children waited for their education.

When we take a nationwide view of the problem we find that of our total population about 11% of Americans are classified as black, but some 16% of the children in public schools are black because a larger percentage of them attend public rather than nonpublic schools and because the black birthrate is higher. Some 1.5% of Americans are classified by the Census Bureau as of Asian or Pacific background, while 6.4% are classed as Hispanic. Only a fraction of one percent are classified as American Indian, Eskimo, and Aleut.

But all these classifications are vulnerable to criticism. A family with a Spanish surname is classifed as Hispanic even though it recently arrived from Madrid, has never lived in Central or South America, and has no Indian ancestry. To assume that all people with Spanish names are disadvantaged, while those with French names are not, is ridiculous, but that is how the government looks at it. The people classifed as "Oriental and Pacific Islanders" differ as much from one another as blacks do from whites. *Black*, as the Census Bureau uses the word, often means a child who genetically is three-fourths, seven-eighths, or fifteen-sixteenths white. Such classifications make no sense at all except as reflections of our history of racial prejudice. Why not just call them all children and send them to the schools where they will get the best education without worrying about establishing a perfect balance?

How far can children reasonably be transported from their homes to achieve desegregation? How shall they be transported? Shall they be reassigned even if, for some, it means transfer to an inferior school? What shall be the penalties assessed against parents who oppose the transfer? These are the questions that create turmoil and divide communities into warring factions.

The problem cannot be solved by hurling the charge "racist" against every parent who objects to having his children transported to a school far across town. The real motives are far more complex. Some parents who believe deeply in racial equality and recognize the need for desegregation are not willing to let their children carry the full burden. Some do not want their children sent to schools so far from their homes that they cannot easily and safely participate in after-school and evening activities. Some fear that disciplinary problems and crime rates will be higher in the new schools, and in many cases there is good reason for their fears. Many parents would oppose cross-town busing even if all the children in all the schools were of the same race.

Although "busing" has become the code word, it is not the real issue. The opposition to reassignment would be just as great if school buses had never been invented — if children had to be transported to more distant schools by their parents, if they traveled by subway, or were expected to walk.

Many liberal congressmen and judges who vigorously support busing as a remedy for segregation send their own children to private schools that are segregated on the basis of socioeconomic class. Their motives for doing this are very similar to those of parents who object to busing. Busing has been ordered by courts and school boards, not because they think it educationally sound, but because they want to comply with the law and have been unable to think of any alternative.

Has busing resulted in better education for black children? Opinions differ, partly because of the great difficulty in measuring educational quality and educational achievement. Those who draw conclusions from their observations of a few schools usually come up with evidence to support the conclusions they previously held. A more comprehensive investigation, with a larger sample, was made by James S. Coleman, who had been commissioned to report on desegregation as required by the Civil Rights Act of 1964. When Coleman's report, *Equality of Educational Opportunity*, was published in 1966 one of his conclusions was that blacks learned more when reassigned to integrated middle-class schools. This was cited in numerous cases in which federal judges ordered busing to integrate the schools.

Nine years later, however, Coleman, in his *Trends in School Desegregation 1968-73*, concluded that one effect of court-ordered busing has been to increase the white exodus from the inner cities. When busing was ordered between inner cities and suburbs, white children who remained in the city were sent by their parents to nonpublic schools. Consequently, forced busing was counterproductive in that it resulted in resegregation.

Disillusionment about busing as a solution is found now among parents of both races. Clarence Thomas, a black educator who is head of the Equal Opportunity Commission and a former Assistant Secretary for Civil Rights in the U.S. Department of Education, has this to say:

> Twenty-eight years after *Brown*, the evidence on minority education . . . provides no reason to believe that busing or proportional representation is the route to educational quality. . . . The controversy over busing has diverted attention away from the educational problems experienced by minorities at the elementary and secondary levels. . . . A recent poll of black parents in the Boston school system reveals an awareness of the futility of adhering to a traditional approach in the face of worsening problems. For the past nine years, Boston has been embroiled in a battle over court-ordered busing.
>
> The controversy has centered on schools generally recognized to be of poor quality. Simply put, black kids were bused from bad schools in Roxbury to worse schools in South Boston.
>
> Although most of the parents of black children involved in this plan support integration as a concept, 79% would prefer a voluntary parent choice system of integration. Another important message contained in this poll is that one does not have to be against civil rights to oppose school busing.[9]

In an essay review of six books published in 1980-81, Vernon Smith says, "Quality education and quality of educational opportunity are concepts and ideals still being redefined more than 25 years after *Brown*. A generation of research has not resolved the issues surrounding these concepts . . . the ends are still right and just, it is the means on which contributors to these six books continue to differ."[10]

Opinions will no doubt continue to differ, but it now seems apparent that court-ordered busing has created turmoil and has interfered with the education of children of all the races involved, without solving the problem. We must find a better way.

1. John Locke, *On the Conduct of Understanding*, Classics in Education (New York: Teachers College Press, 1966), p. 34.
2. Aristotle *Nicomachean Ethics*, vol. 1.
3. Mortimer J. Adler, *The Paideia Proposal/An Educational Manifesto* (New York: Macmillan, 1982).
4. Robert Ulich, *Crisis and Hope in American Education* (Boston: Beacon Press, 1939), p. 28.
5. Eric Ashby, *Any Person, Any Study, An Essay on Higher Education in the United States* (New York: McGraw-Hill, 1971), p. 28.
6. Marsha M. Correll, *Teaching the Gifted and Talented*, Fastback 119 (Bloomington, Ind.: Phi Delta Kappa, 1978), pp. 7, 10.
7. John Gardner, *Self-Renewal* (New York: Harper & Row, 1964), p. 34.
8. *U.S. News & World Report*, 7 February 1983, p. 8.
9. Clarence Thomas, "Equal Opportunity and Federal Policy," *Education Week*, 16 June 1982, p. 24.
10. Vernon H. Smith, *Phi Delta Kappan* 63 (April 1982):570.

5

How Shall Teachers Be Selected, Educated, and Rewarded?

The culture that distinguishes civilized human beings is not transmitted through the genes. It can be lost in a single generation if it is not passed on to children during their formative years. Each of the dark ages that blot the pages of history began when the older generation failed, for one reason or another, to transmit its culture to the young.

Today's children at birth do not differ greatly from their stone-age ancestors — significant evolutionary changes do not occur within so short a span. The brain is neither larger nor more complex; the sense organs are no more acute; and the impulses no better controlled. Yet, within a few years after birth, we expect a child to exhibit all the traits of a civilized adult. Whether he or she will do so depends on education, formal and informal.

The culture of a civilized society — in addition to tools and techniques — includes language and literature, mathematics, science, and the arts as well as customs, beliefs, and social norms. All these must be learned anew by each generation.

In primitive societies the culture is transmitted directly from parent to child, but as a society advances it becomes increasingly difficult for parents to teach their children all they need to know. When a written language develops, children must learn to read if they are to have access to recorded knowledge. Gradually the process of social transmission becomes institutionalized. Schools appear, and with the schools come teachers.

In a complex society, or one in which the rate of social change is accelerated, the responsibilities of teachers multiply. No longer is it sufficient merely to teach children to read and to guide them along established paths. Now teachers must introduce children to a complex world in which many of the paths are not clearly marked and prepare them to live in a future world whose boundaries are yet unknown. This makes teaching the most difficult and the most important of all the professions. With good schools and good teachers our society will survive and flourish. Without them our society will decline.

Teaching as a Profession

Psychology is a science, teaching is an art, and sciences never generate arts directly out of themselves. An intermediary inventive mind must make the application, by use of its originality.[1]

William James

Teaching is indeed an art — a very high art — involving creativity, imagination, intelligence, concern for students, understanding of the nature of the learning process, knowledge of the subject taught, and ability to communicate that knowledge as well as the originality mentioned by William James. Like other arts it requires talents and skills not easily transmitted from one individual to another. But in today's world, teaching is also a profession.

A profession rests upon a substantial body of scholarly knowledge of a kind that requires higher education. Medieval universities prepared men — rarely women, although the story of Portia in Shakespeare's *Merchant of Venice* suggests that there were exceptions — for careers in theology, law, and medicine, plus a fourth — the scholar-teacher who eventually would instruct all the others. The word "doctor" meant scholarly teachers long before it came to mean physician as it now is commonly used — a usage that resulted no doubt from the fact that the physician was often the only person in town with a doctor's degree of any kind. In some countries, however, the teacher was called "master" rather than "doctor" and consequently we now offer both master's and doctor's degrees. The reason for placing the master's degree below the doctor's is lost in history.

When I was in Sydney I once spent an evening with a group of educators, some Australian and some American. An American teacher asked whether teaching was considered a profession in Australia. "Of course," an Australian replied, "It is one of the only two real professions today." He went on to explain that a profession is a vocation chosen by people who are dedicated to their work and who place their contribution to human welfare above their own pecuniary gains.

He contended that law and medicine, as practiced today, are at best only borderline professions because practitioners accept a fee for each service rendered and judge their success and the success of their colleagues on the basis of income. Teachers, in contrast, may spend an extra hour after school helping children and never think of charging a fee or asking for overtime pay. They accept this as a professional duty, because the primary obligation of a professional person is to the students, clients, or patients, not to an employer or administrator. They do their work as well as they can, not because they are required to by an overseer but because they feel obligated to the people they serve.

In nineteenth-century America, however, elementary teachers were rarely considered professional because few of them had any higher education. As recently as 1920 it was possible, in many parts of the nation, for a young man or woman to graduate from high school in the spring, attend a normal school for 12 weeks during the summer, and become a teacher the following fall. Most of the teachers who taught me in elementary school had only this kind and amount of preparation. Typically, the women taught for only a few years, married, and then quit teaching. Obviously they could not be considered members of a learned profession.

High school teachers more often had some college background, many were graduates of liberal arts colleges, and at least a few had received some instruction in pedagogy. In the South, a small-town superintendent of schools who made a lifetime career of his work was often called "the professor." But public school teaching could not be a true profession until a much larger number of teachers were better prepared for their work.

The problem of deciding what is a profession is confused by the fact that the noun "profession" and the adjective "professional" are used in substantially different ways. A professional actor needs talent but has no need for higher education; Shirley Temple was a fine actress at the age of four. We speak of professional football and baseball players, professional gamblers, and even of professional criminals, but this does not mean that they are members of the learned professions. It means only that they are good at what they do and are paid for it.

The requirement of legal licensing or certification does not confer professional status. Lawyers and physicians are licensed but university professors are not. Clergymen need no legal licenses — only the approval of their respective denominations. But barbers, beauticians, and realtors are licensed.

The effort to evaluate the present status of *teaching* or *education* as a profession is made difficult by the fact that these words refer, not to a single occupation, but rather to a cluster of related activities. The profession of education includes supervisors, school and college administrators, and a wide variety of specialists such as curriculum directors, counselors, school psychologists, and classroom teachers of every subject from elementary reading to nuclear physics and philosophy. All these men and women share responsibility for the education of the young, but they differ greatly in outlook, educational background, and their own concept of their roles and responsibilities. They have no well-established channels of communication. No single professional journal is read by all or even a majority. Elementary and secondary teachers and college professors all too rarely confer with one another on professional problems.

While all physicians hold M.D. degrees, and lawyers hold law degrees, teachers and other educators possess a wide variety of degrees: A.B., B.S. in Ed., M.A., M.A. in Ed., M.A.T., Sc.D., Pd.D., and Ed.D. It is difficult for men and women of such varied educational backgrounds to think of themselves as members of the same profession.

Because of its great diversity, it seems probable that teaching will remain a unique profession, less tightly knit and homogeneous than others. Within our profession, diversity is necessary and desirable, even while we continue our efforts to improve education by enhancing the status of teachers.

Salaries

Public school teachers in our affluent nation do not live in poverty but neither do they enjoy many luxuries. As indicated by the table below, their mean salaries have remained only slightly above the mean for all Americans earning salaries or wages:

Historical comparison of salaries for teachers and all other vocations.

	Mean salaries of instructional staff in elementary and secondary public schools	Earnings per full-time employee working for salaries or wages in all vocations in the U.S.
1929-30	$ 1,420	$ 1,386
1939-40	1,441	1,282
1949-50	3,010	2,930
1959-60	5,174	4,632
1969-70	8,840	7,340
1979-80	16,813	14,800
1981-82	19,894	?

Source: *Digest of Educational Statistics, 1981*, N.C.E.S., U.S. Govt. Printing Office, p. 61 (except figures for 1981-82 which are from *Estimates of School Statistics*, 1981-82, NEA, p. 8).

The top salaries for teachers of long experience are, of course, much higher than those listed above. The mean is pulled down by the large number of teachers with only a few years experience. The mean also differs greatly in different parts of the nation. In Alaska the mean salary for teachers was $32,000 in 1981-82. In many Eastern and Southern states it was only half that figure.

Despite inflation, the purchasing power of teachers and other employees has more than doubled since 1930. Almost all Americans are living better. But it should be noted that during the second half of this century the working hours of men and women in most vocations has been reduced while the work week of teachers has not; and in some states the school year has been lengthened.

Although many teachers took a cut in salary during the early 1930s, the cost of living dropped so much that teachers who kept their jobs had an increase in purchasing power. From 1940 to 1970 the salaries of teachers rose faster than the cost of living, but between 1970 and 1980 teacher salaries did not keep pace with the rapid inflation of that decade. Their purchasing power dropped by about 15%.[2]

During this same half century there has been a distinct trend toward equalization of salaries for teachers at the various grade levels. In 1930 nearly all schools paid high school teachers substantially more than elementary teachers, and college teachers received considerably more than high school teachers. Today, elementary and secondary teachers are on the same salary schedule in nearly all school systems. The mean salary for high school teachers is slightly higher because more of them have master's degrees, and they have usually taught longer.

The salaries of college teachers today are no higher than those of public school teachers who hold the same degrees. Although the mean for full professors in major universities is now about $38,000, and in a few institutions much higher than that, the mean for faculty members of all ranks in all kinds of higher institutions was about $26,000 in 1982-3. In many public school systems a teacher can rise to that salary with a master's degree, and with a Ph.D. or Ed.D. may be considerably higher. Consequently, an individual's decision as to whether to teach small children, adolescents, or adults need not be based on expected differences in income.

Even though teachers do not live in poverty, their salaries are lower than those of people in other professions and vocations requiring comparable skills and education. But there is little point in comparing teacher salaries with those of physicians because medicine is a fee-taking profession while teaching is a socialized one. People in socialized professions receive lower pay because their value is determined by someone else; physicians set their own fees and have a considerable amount of control over the fees established as "standard" by the insurance groups that pay medical bills.

Nor is there much point in comparing teacher salaries with those of movie stars or professional athletes, whose worth is judged by the rarity of their talents and the number of people willing to pay to see them perform. An outfielder who can hit 60 home runs a year is highly paid because there are few who can rival his feat and because many people will pay to watch. Television or motion picture stars can demand high salaries because their performances are seen by an enormous audience. Similarly, the author of a book receives royalties based on how many readers are willing to buy it. But teachers, except for those on television, reach only a small audience.

The contention that teachers should accept lower salaries than those in other vocations because of greater job security misses the essential point. Security has great appeal to those of mediocre ability, but to able and enterprising men and women it is of little consequence. They are more concerned about opportunity. A salary schedule that provides security but offers no opportunity for advancement after the age of 40 is likely to attract people of only modest ability.

Some still insist that teachers, like ministers, should renounce worldly goods when they choose their profession — that they should get their satisfaction from the knowledge that they are contributing to the welfare of humanity. Perhaps there were a few such teachers in the Middle Ages but to expect to find two million of them to staff the American schools of today is a hopeless task. Better rewards for superior teaching would attract more talented men and women into our profession.

The Rewards of Superior Teaching

Adults who look back over their student years can easily recall some outstanding teachers who stimulated their thinking, motivated their learning, and raised their levels of aspiration. Unless they were exceptionally fortunate they will recall other teachers who were mediocre in these respects, and some who were downright incompetent. They may be aware that some of their best teachers had the same degrees and the same years of experience as some of the worst. It is very probable that the best and the worst drew similar salaries.

Public school teachers are trapped by salary schedules which, in most cases, are based entirely on degrees and length of service. All receive the same salary as soon as they have the specified degrees and about 14 years of experience. Earning the degree is laborious but not especially difficult for anyone bright enough to become a teacher in the first place; and getting the experience is just a matter of hanging on.

Hanging on requires more persistence than talent. Once teachers gain tenure they are not likely to lose their jobs unless they commit felonies or enrollments drop sharply. Under present laws, rules, and union contracts, administrators find it so difficult to discharge teachers for incompetency that they just give up and let the children suffer. And it would be naive to assume that there is no incompetency among "fully certified" tenured teachers.

No certification requirements can give assurance that every teacher who meets the standards will be competent. No sequence of college courses, no period of supervision, can make it certain that every teacher will have the necessary combination of traits. The best that can be hoped is that better selection of candidates and better teacher education will increase the probability that teachers will have the desired traits and will be able to avoid the mistakes that render teachers ineffective. We do not know how to provide a teacher with the "intermediary inventive mind" that makes a great teacher.

Because of these limitations it is unwise to administer certification requirements rigidly — to insist that *every* teacher must have taken the same courses either in the professional sequence or in the academic disciplines. Nor can we safely assume that requiring more college education will result in better teaching. When good teachers emerge we should welcome them to our profession and not concern ourselves with what courses they took in college.

But we must also reward good teaching and provide for upward movement. Today we do not. By the time teachers are 38 or 40, they arrive at the top of the salary schedule and know they will draw the same pay (except for cost-of-living adjustments) until they retire. At an early age they have bumped their heads against a very low ceiling. And this is true of even the very best teachers. Upward progress has been stopped at an age when people in other professions are just getting started and can look forward to many more years of upward movement.

Teachers of exceptional competence should be exceptionally rewarded — by greater recognition, higher salaries, or both. If they are not, there is great danger that they may be drawn away from the profession by the higher rewards offered in other vocations. This is, indeed, what is happening — what has been happening for a long time.

If we can agree that teaching talent must follow the normal curve of distribution, just as do all other talents, it follows that if only we could identify them — if we could agree on a way of judging talent — we could name the best 30%, 10%, or 1% of teachers in each school system. But because of the ceiling on salaries, these individuals have no more opportunity for advancement than do those of lesser talent. If they become administrators, as some will, their great talent as teachers will be lost to students — a tragic loss — and there is no assurance that they will be equally successful as administrators because administration requires a different combination of traits.

These remarkable teachers should be kept in the classroom and adequately rewarded. Their talents are as rare as the talents of the best actors, writers, musicians, architects, or scientists. But while the best of those in other fields receive higher salaries, and the very best have some chance of winning a Nobel Prize, a Pulitzer Prize, an Oscar, Emmy, or Tony Award, the very best teachers are condemned to obscurity and modest rewards. Their top salaries will be roughly comparable to the top salaries of coal miners, garbage collectors, or those who work on assembly lines. There is something terribly wrong with such a system.

Legislators and school board members — all of whom have been students and know that teachers differ greatly in talent — say they would like to provide higher salaries for superior teachers, if such teachers could be identified, but they say it is financially impossible to raise the salaries of all teachers in order to reward the superior minority. When the issue is raised in teachers' meetings someone is likely to shout, "Merit pay!" as though it were a naughty word. Both AFT and NEA are adamantly opposed to basing pay differentials on merit and insist that they must be based on objective criteria such as degrees and years of experience, because subjective ratings are unreliable.

This effectively precludes any possibility of a true merit-pay play, because the important differences among teachers do not lend themselves to objective measurement. Evaluation must be based on human judgment just as it is when we select a symphony conductor, senator, or president, or when we judge a book, a musical composition, or a work of art. And yet we do make these judgments and distribute rewards accordingly. No one dreams of judging novelists, artists, or musicians by asking how long they have worked or what degrees they held. Teaching, too, is an art.

Teacher unions fear that a merit-pay plan would give administrators more power, and that they would reward docility and conformity rather than quality of teaching. But this can be avoided by taking the decision making out of the hands of administrators and basing promotions on a distillation of subjective judgments from colleagues, visiting scholars, parents, students, and former students.

Of all these, I would place the highest emphasis on the opinions of *former* students who are now adults — those who can look back over their school years and ask themselves which teachers contributed the most to their education. By the time teachers reach the current top salary and are ready to be promoted above that level, some of their former students will be adults. They would be happy to have an opportunity to offer evaluations of their former teachers. Their judgments are essential; fellow teachers, administrators, supervisors, and other visitors have seen the teachers at work for only a few hours, but former students have observed them daily for a year or more. They are the ones whose opinions should be listened to.

The public schools might borrow ideas from colleges and universities, which rank their faculties as teaching assistants, instructors, assistant professors, associate professors, and professors. The pay differentials among these ranks are substantial. In addition, many universities provide named *chairs* for outstanding full professors.

Many colleges evaluate teaching performance before making promotions, though major research universities tend to be more concerned about research and publications. But neither research nor the journal articles of professors can be judged "objectively." They are judged subjectively; and the judgment is every whit as difficult as are judgments of teaching quality. As a result of such judgments, faculty members are motivated to improve their work. Inevitably, some errors are made, but the system is far better than one of keeping all in the same rank throughout their lives.

Public school teachers should also be given titles, as they are in some countries. They might start as *apprentice teacher*, move up to the rank of *instructor*, and then the more talented could aspire to become *master teachers*. Fears that all parents might want their children to have the master teachers could be allayed by means of a team-teaching plan so that each child would have a master teacher for a part of the day.

Would a ranking system cause jealousy? No doubt it would, just as there is jealousy among members of all arts and professions. There is jealousy among college faculty members, but no one suggests that we reduce all professors to the rank of instructor just to avoid it. The occasional jealousy does not seriously damage the educational process.

Pay differentials among the ranks should be substantial. Master teachers should receive salaries higher than those paid to any teacher today. They should be paid as much as administrators in order that the best teachers will not be forced to leave the classroom in order to advance themselves. No one assumes that a hospital administrator must have a higher income than that of the best physicians working with patients in the hospital; and no one should insist that a principal must have a salary higher than that of the very best teachers. In this respect, professions are vastly different from businesses.

Is all this just a dream? Perhaps, for the tide runs strong against it. But I hope the time will come when all professional organizations and teacher unions will make an honest effort to find a satisfactory way of relating pay to quality of work instead of saying it can't be done. If they do not, the profession will continue to lose some of its best teachers to jobs that offer higher rewards. The schools, and the students, cannot afford to lose them.

Unions and the Ultimate Weapon

Industrial and trade unions became an accepted part of the American scene at a time when employees were badly exploited. Miners, industrial workers, seamstresses in clothing factories, and many other employees worked long hours under hazardous conditions for poor pay. Because of the surplus of labor, a worker had no choice but to accept the pay offered. If he protested about wages or working conditions, he was likely to be fired for insubordination.

At the same time, the owners of mines, factories, mills, and railroads were growing enormously rich, built mansions, bought yachts, and married off their daughters to impecunious counts and dukes. It rarely occurred to them that a larger part of their profits should go to those who worked in their shops. Unions were necessary because individual workers were not in a position to demand higher wages or better working conditions, but a union leader representing thousands of workers could make such demands and threaten to close the plant if the demands were refused. By the 1930s a majority of Americans had come to the conclusion that the strike is a legitimate weapon against a private, profit-making industry. Laws were passed to support that conclusion. Union leaders still would prefer to settle disputes by arbitration but insist on the right to strike as a last resort.

In industry and mining, unions were successful in getting higher wages and making work places safer and more comfortable. Wages rose so rapidly that by 1945 or 1950 many miners and semiskilled factory workers had higher incomes than members of the less well-paid professions such as teaching, nursing, social work, and the ministry. Inevitably it occurred to teachers that unionization might be a way of improving the salaries and working conditions of teachers. The movement toward unionization grew most rapidly in school systems where administrators were arbitrary and unwilling to listen to teacher grievances.

But questions persist concerning the appropriateness of unions in nonprofit professions, which receive their support from public funds. In a 1979 editorial in the *Phi Delta Kappan*, Stanley Elam commented, "Even after nearly two decades of experience with collective bargaining, many teachers are still quite ambivalent about it. They are particularly unsure of the value of their 'ultimate weapon,' the strike." My own conversations with, and letters from, teachers in many parts of the country confirm this view.

Parents and other citizens are similarly ambivalent. When asked "Should public school teachers be permitted to strike?" 45% said yes, 48% said no, and 7% were uncertain. The figures are almost identical for those with and without children in school and there were only minor regional differences.[3]

Because unions come into power only when teachers vote to have the union represent them, teachers, when given the opportunity to vote for or against representation, must ask themselves these questions:

1. Are unions successful in getting better working conditions and higher salaries by means of strikes? (Because the evidence from various cities is confusing and conflicting, teachers should evaluate the evidence themselves, instead of accepting the interpretation of someone who is pro-union or anti-union.)
2. Are the long-range gains resulting from a strike sufficient to offset the loss of education resulting from a prolonged strike?
3. Is the principle of collective bargaining less appropriate in a profession than in an industrial job?
4. Is collective bargaining less appropriate in a vocation paid from public funds than in an industry that has profits to divide?
5. If the union establishes a union shop, is it sound policy or ethically legitimate (regardless of the law) to force the dismissal of a teacher who was tenured before the union existed and who, for reasons of conscience or other reasons, refuses to join or to pay comparable fees?

All these questions are in some sense "loaded," but I have tried to state them in such a way as not to imply the answer. They must be asked, and answered, by any teacher facing the problem of whether to vote for unionization.

The Education of Teachers

The nationwide reexamination of the schools that began in the 1950s and continues today led to controversy over the ways teachers are educated. In its initial phase the debate was characterized by such extreme statements that it appeared that the scholars and scientists of the nation were lining up against the educators. Perhaps it was inevitable that the first broadsides should be fired by those most angry and answered by those most vulnerable, but before long, more reasonable and moderate people from both groups began making themselves heard. It became apparent that doubts and uncertainties existed in both groups. The result was a search for solutions.

The disagreements were based on fundamental differences in philosophy rather than on ignorance or malice. They resulted from different concepts of human nature and of the learning process. The conflict is best understood in terms of a thesis and its antithesis, even though few of those involved in the controversy accepted either the thesis or the antithesis in its pure form, and many of us found ourselves torn between the two points of view. But, as a battle of ideas, sometimes between individuals, more often within individuals, the controversy took this form of diametrically opposed views:

The classic thesis in education rests upon these basic premises:[4]
1. Man is dual in his nature. He is a thinking animal, but the fact that he thinks is of far greater importance than the fact that he is an animal.
2. As an animal, man can be studied empirically through the sciences of biology, psychology, and sociology, which can throw light on his responses and some aspects of his individual and social behavior. But man as a thinking being — his most important aspect — is best known through the humanities and a rational approach.
3. Man, in his fundamental nature, is everywhere and at all times the same. The apparent differences are of far less importance than the underlying similarities.
4. Certain periods in human history represent the human mind at its highest peak, and our cultural heritage is best transmitted to the young through the study of the writings and other achievements of these periods.
5. Man possesses free will. He can choose between good and bad, between the valuable and less valuable. He is not a machine.

Acceptance of these premises leads to the
following principles as a basis for formal education:
1. Knowledge of himself, of his past, and of the world about him is available to man and is essential to his best development as a human being. But knowledge is not the end of education; it is a means toward an end. The end is understanding, which is achieved by his ability to reason.
2. Transmission of the cultural heritage is the major responsibility of the schools. It must involve a knowledge of the classics and clear thinking about the ideas in the classics.
3. Basic or liberal education must be sharply divorced from vocational and other forms of specialized education lest it become involved in

practical and mundane considerations, which eventually will sweep it into oblivion. But, since intellectual excellence is the chief good, from which all other goods follow, a liberal education is the best preparation for any vocation because it results in the fullest development of the mind.

4. Because truth itself does not change, liberal education should change but little from year to year or century to century.

5. The curriculum should be organized around the inherent logic of subject matter. In elementary schools the major emphasis should be placed upon learning the skills involved in the use of word and number. Linguistic facility will be stressed at all levels, and the student's knowledge of language must involve the study of languages other than his own.

6. The curriculum must be constructed by those best qualified to know what is best, what is most important, and what logically comes first. The interests of children and of adolescents do not constitute a reliable guide.

7. The teacher must be a scholar, and the better scholar he is the better teacher he is likely to be.

Those who hold to the classic thesis usually deny that the art of teaching can be learned in professional courses in education. They believe rather that the time devoted to such courses could better be given to improving the scholarship of the future teacher.

This classic thesis provided the basis for most formal schooling until well into the nineteenth century. It controls the preparation of college and university teachers today. Except for those in community colleges, it is rare for a college teacher to have had any professional courses in education, and many have not even taken a course in elementary psychology.

Early in the twentieth century a new point of view developed — one that reflected scientific discoveries of the nineteenth century, including the Darwinian view of human origins, as well as the new psychology with its emphasis on individual differences and new methods of testing intelligence, plus the pragmatic philosophies of Charles S. Pierce, William James, and John Dewey.

The antithesis that developed from these converging streams
was a rejection, almost point by point, of the classic thesis:

1. Man, in all his aspects, is subject to natural laws, which are best understood if approached through the empirical sciences including biology, psychology, and sociology.

2. Mind is not a separate entity but an activity or function of the entire organism, especially of the neurological system.

3. Individual differences of many kinds, including learning capacity, are vast and are measurable. In educational planning these differences are more important than the uniformities.

4. Final or positive knowledge is not available to man. Facts are at best statements of probable relationships. We should devote ourselves to finding and using the best available evidence, but new experimental investigations may render this evidence obsolete. Consequently, we cannot proceed from hard and fast premises but only from tentative probabilities.
5. Values are relative and rest upon no absolutes, no a priori truths. The values of another day may not be appropriate for those living today.

A move toward the antithesis became apparent in the late nineteenth century and gained momentum in the twentieth. It was evident in the normal schools and teachers colleges, which began to stress the importance of understanding the nature of children: their interests, their capacities for learning, their limitations, and the ways in which one child differed from others. To those who accepted the antithesis — which was related to, but not identical with, the Progressive movement in education — the goal of education is the "growth" of the individual. But ends are not final; when achieved they become means toward other ends. In the final analysis ends and means are indistinguishable. It follows that education is not preparation for life; education is life itself.

By the 1930s this philosophy had become dominant in graduate schools of education — it was most apparent at Teachers College, Columbia University. Because a great many graduates of this institution became teachers in the single-purpose teachers colleges of the day, it had a controlling influence on the way elementary and secondary teachers were educated.

However, the antithesis never was accepted by those responsible for the education of college teachers, who still were educated in accordance with the classic thesis. Programs leading to the Ph.D. continued to stress scholarship — often in a narrowly delimited academic area — and prepared students to be productive scholars. Although the majority of recipients of this degree intended to become college teachers, they rarely received instruction in the history of education, the various philosophies of education, or the nature of the learning process. It was assumed that if college teachers knew their discipline well and were engaged in discovering new knowledge within that discipline, they could learn on the job how to teach the subject. As a result, a wide gulf developed between the outlook of college teachers and that of elementary and secondary teachers. This gulf was the basis for the controversy over teacher education that began in the Fifties and continues today.

Since 1950 we have moved a long way toward reconciliation of the differences. After the decline of the Progressive movement, professional educators began to reassert the importance of scholarly knowledge for all teachers without abandoning the importance of understanding the nature of the learning process or the need for understanding the school as a social institution. The synthesis that has emerged reflects general agreement on these principles:

1. All teachers, regardless of the subject or age group to be taught, should first become liberally educated individuals with a broad understanding of the major areas of knowledge and free from the limitations of ignorance, prejudice, and provincialism. In the course of their college education they should come to see their own special field as a part of a larger whole and related to other areas of knowledge.

2. In addition, teachers should possess a scholarly knowledge of the subject or subjects to be taught. The scope of their academic major should be consistent with the range of subjects they will teach. Consequently, it should not be too narrowly specialized; it should be a major designed for teachers, not one designed for engineers, physicians, or other specialists.

3. In addition to their liberal education and their major field of specialization, teachers need a background of professional education. (This is a deviation from the classical thesis. Principles one and two above are deviations from the antithesis, but most of those who work closely with teachers now agree on the need for these moves in the direction of a synthesis.)

Although we have not reached full agreement on the kind or the amount of professional education to be required of teachers, there is a fair amount of agreement on the following:

1. Young men and women who plan to become teachers should first give careful thought to the meaning, purpose, and problems of universal public education. Such thinking may be incorporated into a course in educational philosophy, which may or may not follow an historical sequence, or it may be included in a course dealing with the problems of education (such as are dealt with in this book.)

2. Teachers should have the best understanding that psychologists can give them of the nature of the learner and of the learning process, of the nature and extent of individual differences, and of the developmental processes that occur during childhood and adolescence.

3. Before entering the classroom, teachers need some introduction to the methods and materials of instruction. This need not be exhaustive because much of such information will be gained on the job.

4. Teacher education should include a period of practice teaching, cadet teaching, or internship during which a supervisor tries to make sure that the knowledge gained in points one, two, and three above is applied in the actual teaching situation.

Despite the fact that most programs for teacher education now include these four essential elements, we still hear many complaints from students that courses in professional education are dull and uninspiring, and that within the required courses there is much duplication of content. The fact that some of the brightest candidates for teaching are among the complainers is ominous. We should not ignore such criticism. We should take steps to assure that there is no basis for it.

The duplication of content results from course proliferation. A typical middle-sized state university (the one with which I am most familiar) offers 77 separate courses in education at the undergraduate level, plus an additional 87 courses at the graduate level — 164 courses in all. Though each professor can justify the course he or she teaches, duplication of content is inevitable. Obviously no students take all 164 courses — it would require many years of college even if they studied no other subject. They sample from among them, basing their sampling, in part, on a list of requirements. But they take enough courses to hear the same topics discussed repeatedly. The fact that course proliferation is found in other disciplines is a weak defense, though it is true that almost any university department could improve the quality of instruction offered by reducing the number of different courses.

A second problem is quality of teaching. When students encounter a poor teacher in an academic subject, they shrug it off as just one of the hazards of academic life. When they encounter a poor teacher in education they ask, "If he knows so much about good teaching why doesn't he demonstrate it?" Consequently, it is imperative that those who teach the professional courses required for certification be master teachers themselves and conduct classes that are intellectually stimulating. If a university finds it necessary to employ some research specialists who lack classroom competence, those individuals should be given *research* professorships and not be permitted to teach undergraduates, who can be turned away from the profession by uninspired teaching. I am aware that some professors of education are superb teachers and that these are as likely to be found in small departments on obscure campuses as in famous universities. But our schools of education still harbor far too many faculty members whose teaching is mediocre. And the students know who they are.

We must find ways of attracting more students of superior talent into the programs that prepare future teachers. At present the minimal standards for entering such programs are much too low, even in years when there is an oversupply of teachers. Even the best program of teacher education cannot assure quality on the part of its graduates unless those entering the program are carefully selected on the basis of intelligence, scholarship, personality, and motivation for teaching. Even a very modest requirement such as a minimal score of 450 on *either* the verbal or the mathematical portion of the SAT would be a step upward and would do a great deal to offset the current fear that students of inferior intellectual talent are entering our profession.

A school of education could gain national attention, and at the same time enhance the status of our profession, by establishing much higher entrance standards — standards for admission as high as those now found in the better schools of engineering, medicine, and other learned professions. If liberal scholarships were offered, a few such schools — because of their selectivity — would have no difficulty attracting students. Bright students are prone to select the colleges with the highest admission standards. And the graduates of such schools would be in great demand by the schools paying the highest salaries. The scholarships could be provided by funds from the major foundations, the federal government, or by soliciting donations from the people who now are critical of the low entrance standards of schools of education. (I am giving my proceeds from this book to such a scholarship fund.)

The few graduate schools of education that already have rigorous entrance standards do not, in most cases, prepare *teachers*. They give their entire attention to the preparation of administrators, supervisors, and specialists of various kinds. But the greatest need is for outstanding *teachers* of children and adolescents. The major graduate schools of education make little direct contribution to that need.

---

1. William James, *Talks to Teachers*, Norton Edition (New York: W.W. Norton & Co., 1958), pp. 23-24.
2. *The Condition of Education*, NCES, U.S. Govt. Printing Office, 1982, p. 103.
3. Stanley Elam, ed., *A Decade of Gallup Polls of Attitudes Toward Education, 1969-78* (Bloomington, Ind.: Phi Delta Kappa, 1978), pp. 238, 254.
4. This section is an updated version of an address given at the University of Minnesota, 10 December 1954, and published in *Journal of Teacher Education* 6.

6

Why Do These
Problems Persist?

Many of the problems discussed in previous chapters are related to the disagreement over educational goals discussed in chapter 1. Such disagreement is the price we pay for freedom of expression. Better understanding may reduce the intensity but the controversy will continue. We can live with it as long as we are willing to search for acceptable compromises through the democratic process.

Other problems result from the uncoordinated nature of our educational establishment, the cultural and religious diversity of our people, the demand for more and more years of schooling, and the fact that parents have come to expect more than the schools are able to provide. All the problems are intensified by the lack of proper dissemination of information concerning the schools.

The Unsystematic American System

I once had the assignment of assisting a man who had recently been appointed director of education in one of the developing nations and had been brought to the United States by the Ford Foundation for the purpose of learning what he could from our educational programs. He had read widely but had never before been in this country.

He said he would like to start by talking with the "head man." I told him that there was no head man in American education. "But isn't there a U.S. Commissioner of Education?" he asked. I agreed that there was but explained that the commissioner has very little control over our schools. "But who is in charge?" he asked. I had to admit that no one is in charge.

I could understand his bewilderment because in most nations the schools are under the control of a central agency, located in the nation's capital. The chief education officer is often a member of the cabinet, appointed by the chief of state. It is appropriate to speak of the Soviet system of education or the French system for these are national systems and legal entities. Some individual officer or an official group within the national system decides what the goals of the school shall be, what subjects shall be taught, what standards shall be used in admitting students to each level and graduating them from it, who shall be accepted as teachers, and what textbooks shall be used.

The United States has nothing comparable to this at the national level. The U.S. Secretary of Education has little real power or authority except for the distribution of federal funds. When the Founding Fathers wrote our Constitution they left problems of education to the separate states; the word "education" does not appear in the document. As a result we have 50 separate state systems and one for the District of Columbia.

Some states have established firm control over the schools within their borders; others leave many decisions to local communities. Within the limits imposed by the states, schools are under the control of local boards (except in Hawaii where one board serves all schools in the state), which govern units ranging from a single one-room school to those of large cities with thousands of classrooms. There now are some 16,000 such local boards, a number that has dropped from 127,000 within the past 50 years as a result of school district consolidation. Each local board is, to some extent, a policy-making body, although board members often express frustration over the extent that their decision-making power is restricted by state agencies, the courts, and a federal bureaucracy that has provided financial assistance.

As a result of what Frederick Lewis Allen once called "The Unsystematic American System," the chief characteristic of our schools is their vast diversity. States differ widely in their requirements for promotion and graduation, requirements for teacher education, salaries for teachers, and funds made available for education. Even within a state there is great diversity; one city may have very high standards while another has low standards. Although many states have set minimum salaries for teachers, the maximum in some cities is much higher than in others in the same state for teachers with similar qualifications. A high school diploma from one high school may give evidence of scholarly achievement while one from another school — even in the same city — indicates only that the student has been enrolled for four years. Consequently, any statement about American education, or any criticism of it, is probably true for some schools, false for others. Much of the endless debate about the quality of education results from this fact because no observer has an adequate knowledge of all our schools. Each one generalizes only from firsthand knowledge of a few schools.

I would not want it thought that I am proposing a national system of education for the United States. I would oppose it. Even our state systems stifle initiative by imposing too much control. But our lack of a national system does account for much misunderstanding.

There is little doubt that we have some of the best schools in the world, and some of the worst. Some of our teachers are geniuses; others are not as bright or well informed as their students. Some school buildings are magnificent edifices for learning; others are a disgrace to the community. Some schools offer a rigorous academic curriculum; others use a cafeteria approach with something to please every taste. Much of the controversy over education results from this diversity. The debaters are talking about different classrooms, different students, different teachers.

Some problems result from poor articulation of various levels of education: primary, intermediate, secondary, college, and graduate school. Those who construct the college curricula often ignore the fact that some high schools offer courses as advanced as those taught to college freshmen. They require students to repeat these courses, wasting student time. Even when credit is given for high school courses, as is true in foreign languages, most colleges give only one year's credit for two years of high school work. On average, this may be reasonable, but for some students it is not. There is no good reason to believe that a 19-year-old college freshman can learn twice as much in a year as a high school senior who is only a year younger. Advanced placement and early admissions programs have demonstrated that some of the duplication can be eliminated without loss to students, but only a few colleges have such programs.

Graduate education is not well articulated with undergraduate. Students who have majored in a subject during their undergraduate years often complain that the first courses required in graduate school are no more advanced, and no better taught, than those they took as undergraduates. Graduates of the better undergraduate colleges of education often complain, and with good reason, that the courses they are required to take for an M.Ed. in a university duplicate ones they have had as undergraduates. It seems that professors in graduate schools just can't believe that undergraduate courses are adequately taught.

Some problems are exacerbated by the rivalry between public and nonpublic schools. Graduates of independent or church-related schools seem to take satisfaction from each new report of problems in the public schools. They cite the recent study by James Coleman, *Public and Private Schools*, as evidence that their own schools have fewer discipline problems and produce better "cognitive outcomes." Then they offer this rather questionable evidence as a reason for providing vouchers to enable more children to attend nonpublic schools. This angers public school educators, who see their own institutions threatened.

The more prestigious private universities take pleasure in reporting that their graduates have higher incomes and a statistically better chance of being listed in *Who's Who* than do graduates of state universities, preferring to overlook the strong probability that these achievements result more from greater selectivity of students than from better instruction. The kind of students they recruit and accept are more likely to have high incomes regardless of where they go to college, especially if they come from families that can start them off with inherited capital.

In the 1950s highly selective liberal arts colleges such as Swarthmore, Carleton, and Reed took pleasure in calling attention to a study reporting that graduates of these colleges are much more likely ultimately to acquire Ph.D.'s and become academic scholars than are graduates of other undergraduate institutions. They interpreted this as evidence of superior instruction, but a more likely explanation is that these colleges admit as freshmen only students who have the intellectual capacity for graduate work. A college that admits only very bright freshmen will have very bright graduates regardless of whether it teaches them more than other colleges during the undergraduate years.

Cultural and Religious Diversity

As was pointed out in chapter 3, Americans adhere to a wide variety of faiths, Christian and non-Christian; and nearly half are not communicants of any church. The majority of our people think of themselves as members of the white race, but even of these many have some racial mixture in their ancestry if traced back far enough. In 1980 the Census Bureau reported that 26 million Americans were black, but many of these are genetically part white. About 3.5 million are Orientals who can trace their ancestry back to China, Japan, Korea, or Vietnam, but some of these are genetically part white or black. One and a half million are American Indians, while some seven million fall into a category called "all other races." These include Polynesians, Micronesians, Melanesians, Eskimos, and recent migrants from the Near East.[1]

Although we take pride in, and profit from, our diversity, problems of education are more manageable in a nation where all the people share a common cultural heritage, follow the same religion, and are of the same race. People of different backgrounds inevitably expect different things of their schools.

As a melting pot the United States has not been a complete success. For a time the melting pot seemed to work because those who came from Northern Europe and settled in rural communities in the seventeenth and eighteenth centuries intermarried freely and seldom returned to their ancestral homes. They ceased to identify themselves with any European nation, lost interest in their ancestors, and came to think of themselves only as Americans.

But many of the descendants of later arrivals, Italians, Greeks, Slavics, and Serbo-Croats, as well as the Irish who came after the potato famine, have retained their traditions and have divided loyalties. These are the "hyphenated

Americans." Italian-Americans show their loyalty to Italy by becoming defensive when anyone criticizes the Mafia or suggests that Leif Ericsson discovered America long before Columbus. Irish-Americans show their devotion to "the old country" by contributing funds to the IRA and by celebrating St. Patrick's Day.

In the past, our schools paid scant attention to the children's cultural heritage and attempted to move them rapidly into the mainstream of American life. An unfortunate result was that children of immigrants often became critical of the language, clothing, food habits, values, traditions, and lifestyles of their parents and became alienated from them. Now some schools are making greater efforts to enable children to take pride in their diverse cultural backgrounds, but the problem of balancing that emphasis against the need to adapt to American life is a difficult one that is as yet unsolved.

More Schooling, More Problems

Most Americans believe deeply in the value of education and assume that if some is good, more must be better. As a result, the number of years of schooling required has steadily increased. In the early nineteenth century four or five years were considered adequate for most children, but by the end of the century many states required attendance through the eighth grade or until the age of 16.

By 1900 it had become established policy to provide secondary education for all who wished to continue. As a result of growing prosperity, urbanization, and child labor laws, the median years of schooling for young Americans increased from 8.1 in 1910 to 12.5 in 1980. Faced with a growing number of less academically talented students, high schools felt that they had no choice but to lower standards to a level everyone could meet.

Since mid-century a growing number of citizens, including some educators, have insisted that higher education is appropriate for all, regardless of academic talent. The total enrollment in colleges of one kind or another increased from 3.7 million in 1960 to 12 million in 1980. The number of college degrees conferred in 1980 was greater than the number of high school diplomas granted in 1950.

This impressive growth could not have been achieved without some lowering of standards for both admission and retention. Inevitably, a high school diploma now means less than it did when slow learners were encouraged to drop out before graduation. Since the day when "open enrollment" replaced entrance standards in colleges and community colleges, a degree also has less meaning. Even the stronger colleges have experienced grade inflation; "B" has replaced "C" as the average grade. Straight "A" students have become so numerous that graduate and professional schools find it difficult to choose among them. In some colleges more than half the students graduate "with honors." Because of these changes, more years of schooling cannot be assumed to mean better education.

Employers have failed to grasp the implications of universal high school education. Fifty years ago, when only a fourth of all adolescents finished high school, a diploma gave some assurance that the holder had better-than-average academic ability and could easily be trained for a white-collar job. Employers who make such an assumption today may be in for a rude shock, and they will blame the schools rather than the people who have insisted that every adolescent must receive a diploma. The Marine Corps and Army continue to boast that most of their recruits are high school graduates, unaware that graduation has lost much of its meaning.

Parental Expectations

The immigrants who came to America in the seventeenth, eighteenth, and nineteenth centuries were of all social classes, but the majority came from the lower class. In the Old World, opportunity for upward mobility was denied them, however great their talents; but on the frontier, where class lines were less sharply drawn and opportunities more abundant, upward mobility was possible. It became the Great American Dream that children would rise above their parents in social and economic status.

For many, the dream became reality. Sons of serfs became farm owners and often their sons moved to cities and prospered. Sons of day laborers became policemen, clerks, shopkeepers, and skilled mechanics, and some of their children went on to college and entered the professions. Families assumed that each generation would attain higher social status and greater prosperity than the preceding one. Free public education would provide the way.

In the twentieth century the dream began to fade. When more young people received high school diplomas and college degrees, these credentials gave less assurance of upward mobility. Now the son of a factory laborer who receives a high school diploma may find himself back on the assembly line beside his father. The son of a man who became a banker, insurance agent, or business manager with only a high school education now must have a college degree just to replace his father. Boys and girls whose parents are college graduates now need advanced degrees to achieve the vocational level of their parents. Many do not achieve that level. Parents who still expect their sons and daughters to rise above them are likely to be disappointed and to feel that the schools have failed their children.

Parents who are high achievers may no longer expect their children to rise above them, but they still hope their children will equal their achievements. Parents who have demonstrated superior talent in such areas as music, mathematics, or science are likely to expect their children to display comparable talent. An All-American football player expects his son to follow in his footsteps. Physicians frequently expect their sons or daughters to become physicians and assume that they will be qualified to enter medical school. If the youngsters are not qualified, the parents question the quality of the children's schooling and ask, "If we could do it, why can't they?"

But it is inherent in the nature of genetics that children will differ from their parents. Just as some are taller, stronger, and more agile than their parents, others are shorter, weaker, and less agile; some will be more intelligent than their parents and some less intelligent, no matter how intelligence is measured. They will also differ from their parents in the nature of their talents. A parent who excelled in mathematics may have a child who hates the subject and prefers literature. A parent who loves to read may have a child who reads with difficulty and prefers to ski. While educators understand these facts, many parents find them difficult to accept.

In families at the upper end of the scale in any talent, there is likely to be a regression toward the mean with the next generation. Only rarely do the children of geniuses become geniuses. The son of a man who can run the mile in four minutes is not likely to equal that record. A parent who has an I.Q. of 170 is likely to have children of high intelligence, but their scores will not be quite as high as those of their parents.

These facts should not be used to excuse poor schools or poor teaching, but they help explain why intelligent and educated parents are among the most severe critics of the schools.

In dealing with parents whose expectations exceed their children's capabilities, private schools have a distinct advantage over public schools. When Woodrow Wilson was president of Princeton he was called upon by a wealthy dowager who wanted it understood that she was paying the university a compliment by enrolling her son, whom she described as "brilliant and charming," as a freshman. She admitted that her son disliked studying and made low scores on tests, but said she was holding Wilson personally responsible for seeing to it that her boy worked hard and made good grades. After listening patiently, Wilson responded, "Never fear, madam. We guarantee success or we return the boy." Public schools do not enjoy the privilege of returning the boy. If he cannot learn, or refuses to learn, the school must continue to do its best and will be blamed if he fails to succeed.

Informing the Public

People without information are apt to be extremists, whereas those with information are inclined to more moderate opinions.
>						Frank Abrams, former Chairman of the Board,
>						Fund for the Advancement of Education

If everyone were fully informed, educational controversy would not end but its intensity would be greatly reduced. The necessary debates would generate less heat and more light.

An informed person knows that phonics is an essential ingredient in a reading program but does not believe that more emphasis on phonics will solve all reading problems.

An informed person knows that intelligence tests have often been misinterpreted and misused but also knows that such tests, when properly used, are valuable tools that should not be discarded.

An informed person is aware of the need for highly trained mathematicians in our society but does not believe that *every* high school student can master calculus.

An informed person familiar with our tradition of religious freedom will agree that children have a right to pray to the God of their choice but, being familiar with our Constitution, will also know that group prayer cannot be required in public schools.

An informed person knows that young people must be prepared for their life's work (and that most American parents and lawmakers expect the public schools to play a part in that preparation) but will reject the view that all education should be "career education" because life is more than work.

In public debate, an informed educator is at a disadvantage. While an extremist can make dramatic, unqualified charges that command attention, informed people know that their statements must be qualified in such a way as to make it clear what schools, what teachers, and what students they are talking about. They know that any statement beginning "All children, without exception, must . . ." reveals ignorance of the total range of human capacity for learning. Informed people are aware that statements must be phrased in such a way as to allow for these differences, therefore making their prose less vigorous, less effective in commanding attention. Their qualified statements are likely to sound cautious.

While extremists can lash out recklessly against opponents, moderates, because they stand in the center of the arena, must maintain balance while fending off attacks from all sides. Yet it is an essential part of the political process in a self-governing society to resolve conflicts by compromise. The first step toward compromise is informed debate.

The Media

Parents' impressions of their schools are influenced by what they hear from their children, but a large part of what most citizens know about today's education comes to them through television, radio, newspapers, and magazines. These media could contribute greatly to public understanding of the persistent problems of education by providing accurate information, thoughtful interpretation, and calm analysis. But, with occasional brilliant exceptions, media coverage of education is poor in quality, inadequate in scope. All too often the facts are misinterpreted, the analysis is misleading.

Television covers dramatic events that lend themselves to visual messages that can be compressed into a few minutes of prime time. It rarely deals with the essence of education. When college students were in revolt a decade ago, closing schools, threatening and sometimes assaulting administrators, and occasionally looting or burning college buildings, they learned to use television for their own ends. They announced their plans in advance and did not become noisy or violent until the cameras were ready to roll. After watching the events at Berkeley and Columbia, students in other colleges wanted the same publicity for themselves and decided to get into the act.

Although the great majority of students continued to study and to learn, television watchers got the impression that most students were spending their time protesting and had no interest in getting an education. One result was that the public became less willing to support higher education — a problem that continues to plague us long after the protesting students have been replaced by a new and different generation.

Newspapers, with a few exceptions, notably the *New York Times*, which has had outstanding education editors and writers since the time when Fred Hechinger became education editor in 1960, do not give education the attention it deserves. The coverage is spotty, unbalanced, and lacking in depth. One survey of a sample of papers revealed that of all the space given to education 48% goes to athletics, 18% to social activities, and only 34% to everything else — a category that is overloaded with reports of confrontations and disorders.

Editors, eager to give readers what they want, are convinced that everyone wants to know "who won." They know that football and basketball, with all their sideshows — marching bands, cheerleaders, and baton twirlers — lend themselves to photographs that enliven the page. A Latin class is rarely as photogenic as a bevy of cheerleaders in miniskirts or a halfback making a touchdown. Social activities are reported because parents like to see the names of their sons and daughters in print.

But there is another reason for the failure to cover the more important aspects of education. Many editors believe that good reporters can cover any subject — that they can learn about the subject as they go along. Editors assign beginners to cover petty crime, traffic accidents, marriages, divorces, *and* education. Then, after a few months, they move them on to another beat, and eventually to national or international news. But adequate coverage of education requires much more than the ability to report dramatic events. It requires understanding in depth of the problems facing the schools, of the conflicting goals of education, of the history of educational problems, and especially of the statistics used in reporting the results of education. Few reporters have the necessary background, consequently education statistics are frequently reported without adequate interpretation.

The need for knowledge of the history of education was revealed in the 1970s by those who reported the Montessori method as "a dramatic new approach to education." A more knowledgeable reporter would have been aware that the Montessori method has been around for a long time. It was brought to America in 1910 and was taught in many normal schools and used in some schools in the 1920s. And every year or two some bright young reporter comes up with the remarkable discovery that learning how to think is just as important as learning facts — unaware that Socrates came to that conclusion a long time ago.

Statistics from official sources are often misinterpreted. Through the Fifties and Sixties many reporters glibly quoted statistics from the NEA indicating a nationwide shortage of 150,000 to 200,000 teachers. Readers were led to believe that there were that many classrooms without teachers, when in fact there were few, if any. The figures were arrived at by subtracting the number of fully certified teachers available from the number that would be required to take care of growing enrollments, replace those leaving the profession, and reduce class size. In truth, most of the slack was taken up by teachers who were not yet fully certified but many of whom were, nevertheless, perfectly competent. During that period a teacher with an M.A.T. from Harvard who took a job in California could not be fully certified without a course in California history and California school law. Such teachers were counted as part of the teacher shortage.

Publicity given to these misleading figures was partly responsible for the *oversupply* of teachers in the Seventies. Already there are indications that publicity being given to the oversupply of teachers today will contribute to a shortage of teachers in the decades ahead.

Because they have an exaggerated opinion of the power and authority of top administrators, reporters blame school superintendents and college presidents for things not their fault. One city superintendent of schools was sharply criticized in the press because the scores of pupils on a nationally standardized achievement test had fallen sharply within a decade. Ignored was the fact that, during those years, many middle-class families had moved out of the city and had been replaced by poorer families. The test was one that reflected socioeconomic background as much as it reflected the results of schooling. A better informed reporter would have explained the real reason for the decline.

But administrators also get credit when none is due. A reporter eulogizing a retiring president of a state university gave him credit for "building up" the enrollment from 10,000 to 30,000 in 30 years, when in fact the population of that state had grown enormously during those years and state law required the university to accept all high school graduates. The president did not "build up" the enrollment — he just happened to be in the front office while it grew. He could not have prevented it had he tried.

Another reporter said a school superintendent had "hiked" teacher salaries by 85% during his term of office, when in fact teacher salaries all across the nation had risen 110% during these years. A better reporter would have made it clear that the salaries of local teachers were falling behind.

Newspaper coverage reflects the journalistic tradition that news must be dramatic, startling, or at least unusual. When reporters are assigned to cover the education beat, they are prone to look for evidence of disorder or unrest, controversy between teachers and administrators, parental protest about busing, or students smoking pot. These are worth headlines. If there are no dramatic problems to be revealed, they may look for unorthodox styles of teaching. A teacher could get his picture in the paper by standing on his head while teaching algebra. If he teaches in the usual position he will be ignored.

Athletics get better coverage than anything else because sports reporters stay with their subject long enough to become competent. They understand what they write about. Moreover, a breezy, free-wheeling style is more appropriate for writing about sports than for writing about serious educational problems.

Many editors advise their cub reporters to read *Elements of Style* in which William Strunk, Jr., advises writers, "Use the active voice. Make definite assertions. Avoid tame, colorless, hesitating, non-committal language. Omit needless words." For many writers this is sound advice, if used with caution. Journalists, however, have been led astray by Mr. Strunk — they carry his advice to extremes and sacrifice accuracy to style. Their news items — and especially their headlines — abound in strong language and definite assertions: "We are becoming a nation of illiterates," "There is no discipline in today's schools," "Teachers colleges teach nothing but methods," "Children are not being taught to write," "Johnny can't read," "Today's schools are inferior to those of 1900," "Swiss schools are better than ours."

Such statements are strong, forceful, and unhesitating. They appeal to editors because they command the attention of readers. But such assertions, for the most part, are simply not true. They need to be qualified by adjectives such as *many, most, some*, or a percentage, even though the result is loss of vigor. Education writers face the difficult task of retaining a vigorous style while reporting facts accurately. It isn't easy.

The fact that SAT scores fell substantially from 1963 to 1979 was widely reported in newspapers and newsmagazines. Writers, parents, and even some educators interpreted this as evidence of a nationwide decline in the quality of high school education. This was a gross misinterpretation.

The *A* in SAT stands for aptitude — not achievement. This test was designed to measure students' aptitudes for learning in college, not what they learned in high school. It is true that by the time a student reaches high school, aptitude is usually reflected in achievement, but the correlation is far from perfect. If we want to know what students have learned in high school, we should give them achievement tests. And we should give the tests to all students, or to a carefully selected sample of all segments of the school population, balanced geographically as well as across ethnic and racial lines.

SAT scores are based on no such sample. They are not intended to be and should not be interpreted as though they were. Only a third of the high school students in the nation take the test and these are self-selected on the basis of the desire to enter one of the minority of colleges that require the SAT for admission.

In New England, New York, and some other states, from 50% to 69% of students had such desires and took the test in 1982. But in other states the percentage was much lower: 4% in Utah, 3% in Iowa, and only 2% in South Dakota. In my own state most students take the Washington Pre-College test in preference to the SAT, and yet our local papers cite the national decline in SAT scores as evidence that the schools of Washington are failing. Clearly, the people need more accurate information.

Even if the sample were not geographically skewed, it would tell us nothing about *average* high school students because they are not included in the sample. Of those who took the SAT in 1980, 70% were in the top two-fifths of their high school classes; more than 91% had taken four years of English; 67% of the boys and 51% of the girls had taken four years of mathematics; 76% of the girls and 70% of the boys had completed at least two years of foreign language.

Obviously this is a highly selected group. The fact that those taking such academic courses made lower scores in 1980 than those who took it a decade earlier suggests that enrollment in academic courses gives no assurance of superior aptitude, as some scholars have contended. These figures also refute the contention that test scores declined because students were taking more ''soft'' courses. Those who take the SAT are *not* the ones enrolled in easy courses.

The blue ribbon panel appointed in 1976 to investigate the causes of the decline in SAT scores found evidence that between 1965 and 1970 more students with lower grade averages in high school began taking the SAT, but the panel found no evidence of any substantial change in the categories of students electing to take the test after 1970. The test scores suggest, however, that more students of lesser talent *within* each category — rich and poor, urban and rural, black and white, etc. — may have chosen to take the test in the Seventies. The truth is that the Wirtz committee was unable to agree on an explanation for the decline in test scores after 1970. Many hypotheses were proposed — larger families, more broken homes as a result of divorce, increased time spent watching television, etc. — but none was proven. Nor has the rise in test scores since 1980 been explained. There is no evidence of a decrease in broken homes or television viewing since 1980 and yet the scores have begun to rise.

Education reporters should make it clear to their readers that the SAT is not a test of basic literacy or minimal competency; it is a difficult test designed for superior students of high academic talent. Let me cite just one item from the test that is no more difficult than many others. I would hazard a guess that some reporters, as well as some business executives, school board members, and legislators will find it difficult.

City R is 200 miles directly east of city T and city H is 150 miles directly north of T. Assuming that the cities lie in a plane, what is the shortest distance between H and R?
(A) 150   (B) 175   (C) 250   (D) 300   (E) 350

Bright students who understand the Pythagorean theorem and recognize that they are measuring the hypotenuse of a right triangle may see that the ratio 150/200 is the same as ¾ and that this is a 3-4-5 type of right triangle. They will then see that the hypotenuse must be 250 miles.

But this is not a test for slow learners. Failure to find the answer within the time limit may be a handicap for students preparing for some professions but it is not evidence that the schools are turning out illiterates.

A competent reporter writing about the decline in SAT scores would have clarified some of these facts. He surely would have informed readers of the geographical imbalance of those taking the test instead of telling them that the decline gave evidence of a *national* decline in educational quality.

Reports of SAT scores give teachers as well as students a bad name. Many reporters cite SAT scores as evidence that teachers are less intelligent than members of other learned professions. No doubt some are because our minimal entrance standards are lower than those in engineering, law, and medicine; but to draw such a conclusion from SAT scores is a gross misinterpretation of evidence.

The SAT is not given to those who are in a profession or have qualified themselves for it. It is given to high school students. When students take the SAT they are asked to select from a list "the field that would be your first choice in the college curriculum." One of the choices is education. This is very different from asking what profession an individual plans to enter. Bright high school students who want to teach an academic subject — English, history, mathematics, or science — are not likely to check "education" as their choice of subject. They check English, history, mathematics, or science, even though they intend to take such professional education courses as are required for certification. Consequently their scores are not counted among those who plan to become teachers. The only ones counted are those who plan to teach subjects not on the list or those who have a vague interest in becoming teachers but no strong interest in any academic subject.

No one knows how much these facts distort the figures commonly cited, but it seems likely that many of the weaker students who check "education" at the time of taking the SAT will never become teachers. If the tests were given to those who actually enter the profession and become teachers of academic subjects in the public schools, the scores might be much higher. A competent reporter would point this out.

Newsmagazines reporting the decline in SAT scores made the same errors as newspapers — probably for the same reason. Editors of newsmagazines also are prone to assign inexperienced reporters to education. They defend the practice by saying that men and women just out of college have firsthand knowledge — from a student's point of view — of today's schools, but they do not yet know enough about anything else to write about it.

When I was at *Saturday Review* I was visited by a clean-cut young man in a Brooks Brothers suit, who had just received such an assignment. He had recently graduated from an Ivy League college, where he had won a Phi Beta Kappa key, and before that he had attended a famous prep school. He had traveled in Europe but had not been west of Philadelphia. He had never been inside a public school, but he wanted to be a journalist and his editor had told him that education was a good place to start.

In eager preparation for his new assignment, he had read *Blackboard Jungle*, *Why Johnny Can't Read*, and something by Admiral Rickover. He was unaware of professional journals of education. When he asked why so many teachers were on strike, and I suggested that he talk with someone at AFT or NEA, he had to ask what the initials stood for. He wanted to visit a teachers college and was surprised to learn that such single-purpose institutions had just about disappeared from the American scene. He had heard about some of the problems of big-city schools but knew nothing about schools in small towns or rural areas.

Despite my best efforts to help him, his first pieces of writing were full of blunders. He expressed alarm at the discovery that half the children of the nation fall below the norm on achievement tests. But he read his mail, visited many schools, talked with teachers, and began to learn a great deal about education. He was a fast learner and over the next few months his articles improved. Unfortunately, as soon as he began to demonstrate some degree of competence he was transferred to another section of the magazine that the editor considered more important, while another fledgling reporter was assigned to education.

That was 20 years ago. Has the coverage of education in national newsmagazines improved since that time? To find out I looked through recent issues of the three major ones: *U.S. News & World Report*, *Time*, and *Newsweek*.

U.S. News rarely gives much space to education but their cover story for the issue of 17 May 1982 carried the scare headline, "ARE WE BECOMING A NATION OF ILLITERATES?" The story inside clearly implied that the answer is *yes*, and much of the blame was attributed to poor schools and poor teaching. Then, only four issues later, they reported, "Forty-six percent more books were sold in stores in 1981 than five years earlier and the biggest gains were registered by hard-cover editions and more expensive paperbacks." Since illiterates do not purchase that kind of book, it appeared to me that one of the statements must be in error. When I wrote to the editor to ask which, he replied that he saw no discrepancy.

The problem was the headline, which led readers to erroneous conclusions. The word *becoming* implied that the number of illiterates is growing, whereas the evidence is that illiteracy has declined steadily for the past two centuries. A *nation* of illiterates would be one in which a majority could not read nor write. We neither are, nor are we becoming, that kind of nation. The truth is bad enough. Functional illiteracy is indeed a problem for some segments of our population. There was no need to exaggerate. It should be added that the editor, rather than the writer, was responsible for the headline. Editors decide what will go on the cover.

Time frequently gives a part of a page to education (no more than 1% or 2% of the space available for all subjects), and *Newsweek* has a page on the subject in every other issue. But about three-fourths of their pieces in the past six months have dealt with higher education institutions. Most of the few recent pieces on elementary or secondary education are spot-news items dealing with unusual schools rather than with the national scene. One could read all three newsmagazines regularly without gaining much understanding of the real problems of education or of what is going on today in the nation's schools.

The news is available for those who want it. *Education Week* provides excellent coverage of developments in elementary and secondary education; *The Chronicle of Higher Education* does the same for higher education. Unfortunately, neither is read by a sufficient number of people outside the profession, nor by nearly enough classroom teachers.

The weekly magazines gave more attention to education 30 years ago than they do today. *Life*, which was then a weekly, in its issue of 16 October 1950, gave an entire issue of 150 large pages to education and dealt with schools in Oregon, Arkansas, Illinois, Missouri, and North Carolina as well as the Northeastern states. The cover girl was a 15-year-old sophomore honor student at New Trier High School. Some of the articles were unfairly critical — one on teachers colleges was written by a novelist who apparently had never looked at a teachers college anywhere west of the Hudson — but there was a good article on "The Educated Man" by Jacques Barzun; one titled, "A Good High School in Illinois"; one on great teachers; and a fine guest editorial by Henry Steel Commager titled, "Our Schools Have Kept Us Free." There was also a report of a Roper Survey, "What U.S. Thinks About Schools."

In recent years, no magazine reaching a large audience has given that kind of attention to education. Perhaps one reason is that they no longer employ education editors. In the 1950s Terry Ferrer was listed on the masthead of *Newsweek* as "Education Editor." Today, no education editor is listed on the masthead of any of the three major newsmagazines. Presumably, assignments related to education are passed around among various writers, none of whom specializes in education.

Monthly magazines can give writers more time and space for calm analysis and they are not limited to photogenic subjects. They can, if their editors wish, publish articles by authors who are well informed and qualified to make judgments concerning education. But very few do. *Reader's Digest*, with a circulation of 18 million, reaches more parents than any other magazine and could help to keep people informed about the problems of education. But in a review of six recent issues I can find only one article about schools, and that deals with pot-smoking rather than education.

The quality magazines have more space for interpretation but they give far less attention to education than they did a generation ago when Frederick Lewis Allen was editor at *Harpers*, Edward Weeks at *Atlantic*, and Norman

Cousins at *Saturday Review*. The reason for this is unclear. Editors who say that their readers are not interested in education are ignoring the evidence. *Saturday Review* more than doubled its circulation during the ten years it published a monthly supplement on education — circulation grew from 250,000 to 620,000.

Misleading and inaccurate media coverage has contributed to the present low morale of teachers. When teachers were asked in 1971 "Suppose you could go back to your college days and start over again . . . would you become a teacher?" 74% said they "certainly would" or "probably would." When asked the same question in 1981, only 46% gave the same answers.[2] When asked what had a negative effect on their morale, 66% mentioned "Public attitudes towards the schools" and 60% said "Treatment of education by the media."

It is difficult for teachers to take pride in their profession when they know that the public is being told by newspapers and newsmagazines that teachers are less intelligent than members of other professions, that today's children are not learning what they should, and that public schools are inferior to private and parochial schools. Teachers may know that all these facts have been misinterpreted by the press, but they also know that because people have been told these things over and over again they believe them.

To correct erroneous misinterpretations, our nation needs a good monthly magazine — one reaching large numbers of intelligent citizens outside as well as inside the teaching profession — that deals as thoroughly and as competently with education as it does with national politics, international relations, economics, science, literature, and the arts. No existing magazine serves this purpose. Much of the criticism of the schools appears in the popular press, while the analysis and interpretation appears in professional publications written by educators, for educators. The fact that few people outside the profession read both sides contributes to the persistence of educational problems.

---

1. *Statistical Abstract of the U.S. 1981*, p. 33ff.
2. *Condition of Education*, 1982 Edition, NCES, p. 104.

7

Retrospect: The Education Of an Educator

Any book on American education — unless it is strictly a research report — reflects the author's familiarity, or lack of familiarity, with our vast range of educational institutions, small and large, rural and urban, public and private, located in various parts of the country. It reveals the author's awareness, or lack of awareness, of the history and changing philosophies of educational institutions and of the available psychological knowledge of the learning process. But the tone of the book is also influenced by the author's personal experiences as a student, a teacher, and in some cases an administrator, parent, or taxpayer. It is because we differ in all these respects that we come to different conclusions.

My favorite professor, when he caught himself relating another personal anecdote, apologized, "I hope you will forgive me for talking so much about my own experiences but mine, you see, were the only experiences I ever had." Before concluding this book I would like to relate some of the experiences that have given me insight into the teaching-learning process. A large part of what I now know, or think I know, about teaching results from these rather than from anything I have read or was taught in college classes.

***

I began teaching at the age of 20 in a two-room school at Rocky Ridge, Ohio, where I taught grades 5 through 8. Near the school was an abandoned stone quarry where children often played during the lunch hour. One afternoon they returned with a "funny shaped rock" they had found. I knew very little about geology but enough to recognize a trilobite. I also knew that the rocky ridge that gave the village its name was of Ordovician limestone. I explained as best I could what the fossil was and how it got there. All the children were interested. They had been unaware that the land on which they lived had once been under the sea and that the fossils, which many of them had seen, had once been living creatures. They wanted to know more.

We had an encyclopedia and a Book of Knowledge and I found a few books on geology. We read everything we could find about the geology of northwestern Ohio. The students learned not only that the region had once been under the sea but that much more recently it had been covered by glacial Lake Whittlesey — an enlarged Lake Erie that shrank when the glaciers receded.

The next day all the children went to the quarry and returned with a box full of fossils of various kinds. With the help of the books, they identified many. The entire group took part; fifth-graders were as interested as eighth-graders. For the next two days grammar, arithmetic, and the other subjects had to wait while we all studied geology.

Years later I had a letter from a man who had been a pupil in that group. He had become a geologist and attributed his interest in the subject to his early encounter with a trilobite. (Incidentally, not a single parent complained that I was teaching "evolution." But that was in a more enlightened era — 1928.)

Perhaps because of that experience I have never liked rigid schedules that tell a teacher what must be taught and when. The national head of the French school system once boasted to an American visitor that, by looking at his watch, he could tell exactly what every 12-year-old in France was studying at that moment. I would not care to teach in his system. But some teachers impose rigid schedules on themselves. I recall one sweet old lady who taught European history. When it was announced that the school would close for two days because of bad weather, she gasped, "Why, my students will miss the entire thirteenth century."

I prefer a looser schedule that allows me to seize upon opportunities to make learning exciting. This experience also convinced me that teachers can offer elementary instruction without a scholarly background in the discipline if they are willing to join the students in their search for knowledge.

* * *

Because there was no principal at Rocky Ridge I had to make decisions on my own. One seventh-grade boy was brighter and better informed than anyone in the eighth grade. He was also larger and more mature. He was bored with school because nothing he heard discussed was new to him. He told me he wished he could get out of grade school and go to high school in the village a few miles away.

I knew that there was a county rule prohibiting grade-skipping, but after talking with the boy's parents, who agreed that he would be better off in high school, I decided to ignore the rules. At the end of the year I gave the boy a diploma saying that he had completed eight grades.

No one ever caught up with the violation. The boy did well in high school and later in college. Both he and his parents were grateful. I have no regrets about breaking the rules.

* * *

Going back to my own childhood, when I was 4½ years old, Santa Claus brought me a set of blocks, each with a picture of an animal on one side and the name of the beast on the opposite side. On the other four sides were the first letter of the name in script and print, capitals and small letters. The game was to look at the name and guess what animal was pictured on the opposite side.

The first word I learned to read was ELEPHANT. Other words — COW, DOG, CAT, etc. — were not so easily distinguished, but ELEPHANT was the large name of a large animal. Learning the other words took a little more time and closer examination. Rudolph Flesch would not like this because I learned to read many words before I had studied phonics. But it worked.

* * *

At about the same age I had a large map of the United States, mounted on a board and cut out along state lines, like a jigsaw puzzle. I soon learned to put it together and in the process came to see each state as a gestalt and to see its relation to the other states. All these patterns remain firmly fixed in my memory and have been of great help to me in driving around the country and locating places I have read about. If I am asked "What state lies north of Wyoming?" I have no need to go through the nonsense of "bounding the states." I need only look at my mental map and I see Montana. My only confusion is about the boundaries of some of the smaller Eastern states, which were left attached by the puzzle makers because they were too small to cut into separate pieces. I still am vague about these.

* * *

None of the teachers who taught me in elementary school had much professional preparation or higher education of any kind. Several were 18-year-old girls who had graduated from high school in the spring, attended a normal school during the summer, and then returned as teachers the following fall.

Despite their lack of preparation, some of us learned to read easily and well, while others in the same class read very poorly. Some of us became adept at arithmetic, while others, taught by the same teachers, learned to hate the subject. Some students (mostly girls) learned to write beautifully while others — of whom I was one — never learned to write legibly even though we performed all the same exercises as prescribed by the Palmer method of penmanship.

This leads me to think that the achievements of students may depend much more on what they bring to class in the way of special talents and motivation than on the quality of the school or the skill of the teacher. Some students from even the poorest schools achieve greatly; some from the best schools achieve nothing.

* * *

Perhaps this chapter should have been titled, "Confessions of an Educator." Anyway, at this late date, I want to ease my conscience by confessing that I rarely did much homework while in high school. I did read a great deal during the evenings — several books a week — but these were not "homework" because they were not assigned by teachers. Some were trivial but others were good historical novels, books of travel and exploration, poetry, biography, geography, science, and a great deal of history.

Some of my classmates had no time for such books because they were busy every evening doing their homework in Latin and algebra. They made better grades in these subjects than I did — a fact that might have been a handicap if I had planned to enter a highly selective college.

I sometimes wonder what I might have accomplished in later years if I had done my homework. I'll never know, but I am glad I read those books during my adolescent years. They enriched my life and broadened my horizons. And I still have doubts about the kinds of homework most commonly assigned. I would like to see more work and less play during the school hours and more time for leisurely reading at home. The television set does have a turnoff button.

* * *

In an earlier chapter I mentioned the currently widespread belief that all boys and girls should graduate from high school because "dropouts" are destined for a life of poverty, unemployment, and crime. Not always. When I was in grade school my best friend was a boy named Buck who lived on a farm. He milked four cows each morning before coming to school and did a man's work during the summer.

When Buck entered high school he soon found that formal education was not to his taste. He dropped out after a few months and returned to the farm. Some 40 years later, while visiting the scenes of my childhood, I went to see Buck. He owned a large and prosperous farm, had combines and other machinery in his sheds that must have cost a half-million dollars, and had a Cadillac in the garage. (I, with my Ph.D., was driving an elderly Ford.) Buck was planning to retire soon and expected to spend his winters in Florida where he had bought a second home.

So much for dropouts. I do not begrudge Buck his success; he earned it. He always worked harder than I did and he had talents of his own — he was very good with animals and machinery. Neither do I think he made a mistake in dropping out of high school. He has had a good life.

Dropouts from urban schools are, of course, less fortunate. They have not undergone the discipline of farm work nor have they learned a vocation from their parents. Still, I doubt that much is gained by forcing them to remain in school if they lack both the interest in school work and the talent for it. We must find a better solution.

* * *

When I was teaching English at Rossford, an industrial suburb of Toledo, we gave all seniors the Ohio State Intelligence test. This was a test widely used at that time as a basis for college admission.

To everyone's surprise, a boy named Ricardo scored in the top one percentile for college freshmen. Not one of his teachers had previously recognized Rick as a boy of superior talent, but after the test scores were available we gave him more attention. We learned that his father was a puddler in the local glass factory who had brought his family over from Italy only a few years earlier and that no English was spoken in the home. Despite that handicap, Rick had learned to read English well but, because his spoken English was awkward, he was reluctant to speak up in class and he did poorly on essay tests.

We gave Rick more encouragement and helped him get a college scholarship. He majored in mathematics and later became an engineer. Had it not been for the intelligence test he probably would have become a puddler in the glass factory.

* * *

As a teaching assistant at Ohio State I taught educational psychology under the direction of Sydney Pressey, who invented a teaching machine long before Skinner ever thought of it. His machine presented a question with four answers. The first question might be "What is the capital of Ohio?" and the possible answers: CLEVELAND, CINCINNATI, COLUMBUS, TOLEDO.

If a child pressed the bar for TOLEDO nothing happened. When he pressed COLUMBUS a bell rang and the next question appeared. Pressey said the machine had the characteristics of a good teacher. The immediate reward for a child who came up with the right answer was the knowledge that it was right. The machine did not scold or criticize when the answer was wrong; it just sat there waiting patiently for the right answer. Children who came into the laboratory would play with the machine by the hour seeing who could get through the 48 states first.

The machine didn't catch on because this was in the heyday of progressive educators who charged that the machine taught "nothing but mere facts." At that time no one dared ask, "What is so mere about a fact?"

* * *

For those who want adventure, teaching offers many opportunities. Students I have known have become teachers in Nigeria, Kenya, Kuwait, and

113

various South Pacific islands. I have yet to talk with one who has any regrets about not returning to teach in his or her own hometown.

One of my students, Charmaine Wing, typed a book manuscript for me, so we became well acquainted. After she married and had two children, she and her husband decided they would like to teach in Alaska. They found jobs in an Indian-Eskimo village near the Arctic Circle, where she taught the first three grades and her husband taught the next three. There was no high school.

They had a great time. They loved the country, the northern lights, and the people. When the temperature dropped to 60 degrees below zero, that was an adventure. Parents would bring them a 20-pound trout or a hind quarter of a moose as a gift. During school hours their own small children were cared for by a motherly Eskimo woman who made mukluks and parkas for them.

Their salaries were higher than those in the states (Alaska was a territory at that time), and with housing provided for them and no place in the village to spend money, they came out in the spring with a substantial amount of savings.

After a year or two they moved to the Aleutian Islands for variety. I don't know where they are now, but the last time I heard, Charmaine's husband was principal of a school in Fairbanks. I hope they will read this anecdote and write to me.

* * *

The difference between a bureaucrat and an administrator is that the bureaucrat knows all the rules and insists that they be followed in every case, because "if we make an exception in your case we shall have to make exceptions for others too." A good administrator, on the other hand, knows there are times when the rules should be waived or ignored to avoid harm to individuals, or because of special situations.

When I was a teaching assistant at Ohio State University my advisor, Henry Goddard, wanted to go away for the summer and asked me to teach the classes that had been assigned to him. I was delighted because they were upper-division courses and my experience in teaching them would look good on my record when it was time to look for a job. But after Dr. Goddard had left town someone from the registrar's office called me to say that I couldn't teach the courses because the rule book said that teaching assistants could teach only lower-division courses. I went to see Dean George Arps. He pondered the problem, then said, "Yes, we do have such a rule — I made it myself — but, hell, rules were made to be broken. Go ahead and teach the classes. I'll fix it up with the registrar."

Arps was an administrator — not a bureaucrat.

* * *

After one of my professors at Ohio State had delivered a brilliant lecture on a difficult subject, an admiring student asked, "Sir, how long does it take to prepare a lecture such as that?'' The professor, who may have planned his remarks while strolling to class, scratched his head and responded, ''Oh, about 40 years.''

It was an honest answer because the subject was one that the professor had been investigating throughout his long career. His lecture drew upon his own research, the publications of other scholars, and his own thoughtful analysis and interpretation illustrated by anecdotes drawn from his own experiences.

I thought about that incident recently when I received a questionnaire from a legislative committee attempting to find out whether university teachers spend a sufficient amount of time on their duties. We were asked to state just how many hours we spend each week ''in direct contact with students,'' teaching, counseling, preparing for class, in research and writing, committee work, etc. (It failed to ask how much time I spend answering silly questionnaires.)

I have completed many such forms over the years, but always with tongue in cheek because I haven't the slightest ideas what the correct answers are for anything other than classroom teaching. While writing a book or preparing for a class I often write a few pages and then go out to mow the lawn while still thinking about and preverbalizing what I shall write next or what I shall say to the class. Much of the reading that I do for pleasure contributes to what I may say to the class tomorrow. There is no possible way to estimate just how much of the time of any teacher is devoted to professional activities, because these activities become a part of life. Trying to judge teachers' workloads by asking how many hours they spend in front of a class is comparable to judging the workloads of ministers by asking how many hours they spend in the pulpit or that of lawyers by asking how many hours they spend pleading before the bar. Professional people have other responsibilities that do not lend themselves to precise measurement.

* * *

While working for the Ford Foundation I learned how ''prestige universities'' get that way. I was talking with the president of one such institution about a grant he had asked for, when his secretary interrupted to say that the dean and the chairman of the physics department were eager to see him as soon as possible. He told her to send them in. I got up to leave but he asked me to stay, saying he would give them only a minute.

The chairman told the president that they had a young man as guest professor for the summer who was doing significant research on the frontiers of science. The chairman was convinced that this was one of the most remarkable young scientists he had ever met and he wanted to hire him on a full-time basis, but would have to make him a full professor (at the age of 28) and offer a high salary because he was getting other offers.

''If he is that good why doesn't his present university promote him?'' the president asked. The chairman explained that the man was teaching at a university that had a rigid salary and promotion policy, which made it impossible for them to give him a full professorship for another five years.

"What salary does he want?" asked the president. When the chairman named a figure, the president gasped. "Why, that's more than you get." "I know," said the chairman, "but I'm not a genius. This boy is. He will bring fame to our university."

"Very well," said the president, "Get him. I'll find the money somehow." (I happened to know that *average* salaries at the two institutions were comparable, but this one was willing to pay more for exceptional people.)

Five years later "the boy" was nominated for a Nobel Prize. The university gained still more prestige. The other university still clings to its rigid promotion policy and remains obscure.

✻ ✻ ✻

Some Final Thoughts

I have observed that the only college teachers who never complain about their heavy teaching loads are those who first taught in high schools where they were responsible for five, six, or seven classes a day or in elementary schools where teachers are required to be with children throughout the day — even during the lunch hour.

Such loads greatly decrease the probability that a teacher will come to class adequately prepared. Preparations made the night before do not take the place of preparation just before each class. The quality of teaching could be improved by giving teachers time before each class to collect their thoughts and organize their plans.

Team teaching can make this possible if the team includes teacher aides and other assistants to free teachers of responsibilities that do not require professional training. Just as a physician does not change hospital beds or keep his own financial records, a professional teacher should not be expected to collect the milk money or help children with their coats and rubbers. A motherly teacher aide, without professional preparation, can do these things just as well and can also provide the necessary supervision during recess and the lunch hour, giving teachers time for preparation as well as for rest and relaxation.

✻ ✻ ✻

The current emphasis on quality in education results in frequent demands for more "hard work" on the part of students — a phrase often interpreted to mean doing more exercises or solving more problems of the same kind. But that kind of hard work does not ensure quality — quality is achieved only when a student is led to think more deeply about more important things — to ask more basic questions and to pursue their answers more diligently.

✻ ✻ ✻

Education does not lend itself to mass production. Students are not interchangeable units, nor are teachers. Each must be treated as a unique individual.

As a school system grows, the multiplying echelons of administrative authority increasingly separate the policy makers from classroom realities. The administration becomes more bureaucratic, more concerned with promulgating and enforcing rules and regulations, more likely to make "studies" of problems than to solve them. And the cost rises.

If I were a child today, facing 12 years of public school, I would rather take my chances with a school located in a small city or rural village than in any vast metropolis. A Gallup Poll found that most Americans agree. When adults were asked, "Do students get a better education in schools located in small communities or those located in big cities?" 68% said small communities, 21% were uncertain, and only 11% said big cities. The vote was about the same from those living in communities of various sizes. Even big-city residents do not like big-city schools.

There are limits to the purported advantages of school consolidation. Although I had great admiration for James Conant, I think he was mistaken in recommending that no high school should be smaller than 400 students. I would prefer that no high school be *larger* than that size, because a larger school loses the sense of community essential to good education. This is more important than having a complex and diversified curriculum.

For the same reason I prefer small colleges. In a university each professional school is likely to be small — a medical school rarely has more than 400 students — but the undergraduate college becomes so large that the sense of community is lost. Large academic departments may offer stronger majors, but few faculty members are concerned about the total education of a student and consequently a student can get a liberal arts degree without getting a liberal education.

This is particularly unfortunate in colleges that prepare teachers. When Western Washington University was a single-purpose teachers college, every graduate had at least one solid course in world history, one in American history, one in geography, and two or three in literature. Now that Western is a university it is possible for students — by choosing among the "distribution requirements" — to become teachers in a self-contained classroom without a single course in geography or history if they prefer to take other courses in "related areas." Nevertheless these teachers will be teaching both history and geography. The same neglect may be found in other universities.

* * *

When old-timers cite the McGuffey Readers as evidence that our grandfathers got a better education than today's children, educators laugh off such protests as nothing more than nostalgia and insist that the textbooks used today are far superior.

After looking over a copy of the 1879 edition of *McGuffey's Sixth Eclectic Reader*, I am not quite so sure. This book, which was used by millions of Americans in the nineteenth century, contains selections from 111 authors — prose selections from authors such as Addison, Dryden, Bacon, Blackstone, Ruskin, Irving, Jefferson, Holmes, Parkman, Prescott, Macaulay, Thackeray, and Webster, as well as poetry by Milton, Shakespeare, Coleridge, Wordsworth, Tennyson, Bryant, and Longfellow.

In a foreword to the Signet reprint, Henry Steele Commager comments:

> What is striking about the Readers was that they made so few concessions to immaturity. There was no nonsense about limiting the vocabulary to familiar words . . . no effort to be entertaining. There was no drawing back from the harsher experiences of the grown-up world . . . they drew generously on modern English classics and on such American books as might be supposed to be classics, and they took for granted that the young would understand them or that the teachers would explain them — something publishers never appear to think of today.[1]

I have no doubt that many of the selections were too difficult for some of the children who read them, but they had the great virtue of introducing great literature to brighter children, many of whom had no opportunity for education beyond the elementary school level. My father, whose only formal schooling was in a one-room country school, could, and often did, quote long passages from poems and orations that he could only have learned from the *McGuffey Readers*. His pleasure in such literature was obvious and for this McGuffey deserves credit.

The textbooks used today are better adapted to the needs of slow learners but provide less enrichment for highly intelligent students who are ready for serious literature while still in elementary school.

* * *

The effort of some textbook writers and publishers to judge the difficulty of a text by measuring the length of words and sentences is psychologically ridiculous. "Tuscaloosa is a city in Alabama" is a clear sentence containing a simple idea even though the words are multisyllabic. "To be or not to be" is a much more difficult concept, even though the sentence consists entirely of words of one syllable.

* * *

Legislatures sometimes get in beyond their depth. Some states now have laws that teaching certificates may not be denied on the basis of "physical or mental handicaps." Since the term "mental handicap" is often used as a euphemism to cover a wide range of disabilities, including what once was called "feeblemindedness," a literal interpretation means that feebleminded men and women cannot be denied teaching certificates. And some judges are extremely literal in their interpretations.

* * *

William James once observed that the chief use of statistics is to refute the findings of other statisticians. Although I would not go quite that far, I must admit that I now have much less confidence in statistical findings from educational research than I had when I was younger. Statistical significance between two variables indicates that the difference cannot be explained by chance but does not tell us whether the difference has educational or social significance.

When I read a statement beginning, "Research proves that . . ." I become skeptical. Research proves nothing until someone interprets it, and frequently not even then. Research in education is much less definitive than in physics because of the greater number of variables and because some of the variables do not lend themselves to precise measurement.

* * *

Some of the "minimal competency" tests now used as a basis for high school graduation measure only skills that should have been acquired before leaving elementary school. Because they do not measure what is taught in high school, such tests give no assurance that a boy or girl who makes a passing score can perform at the level expected of high school graduates. They should be given at the eighth-grade level; a high school diploma should be evidence of something more.

* * *

Until recently, many university professors, including nearly all professors of education, got their start as teachers in the public schools — an experience that enabled them to see education as a total process from the first grade onward. Now, a growing number, even of professors of education, have had no teaching experience below the college level. Their greater scholarly knowledge of their specialties — educational psychology, educational philosophy, or the history of education — does not fully compensate for lack of classroom experience with younger adolescents and children. The quality of teaching in schools of education might be improved if certification requirements were interpreted with greater flexibility in order to make it easier for those who want to become professors of education to gain teaching experience at each age level before they attempt to teach future teachers. And the presence of these future professors of education in the public schools — if only for a few years — might improve the quality of public school teaching.

* * *

Students are the ultimate judges of a teacher's work. Socrates would be unknown today were it not for a student named Plato who made his name immortal. Mark Hopkins would have been forgotten had not a student named James Garfield said of him, "Give me a log hut with only a simple bench, Mark Hopkins on one end and I on the other, and you may have all the buildings, apparatus, and libraries without him."

Students always evaluate their teachers and share these evaluations with friends and parents. This being the case, it seems obvious that teachers should want to know what their students are saying about them. And yet, many teachers object strongly to student evaluations, thereby keeping themselves in ignorance and denying themselves the best opportunity for improving their work.

It is true that teacher evaluation questionnaires used by some schools include silly or trivial questions and weigh these as heavily as the significant ones. After experimenting with many such forms I have concluded that the best is the simplest. At the end of each term I ask students for anonymous responses to just two questions:

1. What is your judgment of the quality of instruction in this course?
   Circle one: A B C D F
   (If letter grades are good enough for students they are good enough for teachers.)
2. What suggestions do you have for improving the course?

The second question yields a variety of answers from which I learn of my mistakes and inadequacies as well as student reactions to the examinations used, the papers assigned, the reading required, and the balance between lecturing and student discussion.

I have kept such records of student reaction for many years. Now that I am well past the conventional retirement age, the judgment of students is especially important. When the ratings decline I'll know it is time to quit. If my ratings are not higher than those of teachers with far less experience than mine, I *ought* to retire.

✽ ✽ ✽

Unless the students now entering college change their plans, we shall face a teacher shortage of mammoth proportions within a few years. In 1982 a national profile of freshmen reported that 3.0% planned to become elementary school teachers, 1.75% planned to become high school teachers, and only 0.2% planned to become college teachers. Many more than that will be needed.[2]

These students' decisions reflect the oversupply of teachers in the late Seventies but are unrealistic in terms of the *future* need for teachers. The availability of jobs depends, in part, on the number of teachers retiring each year, and because a large number of teachers are now in their forties and fifties, the number of retirements will soon increase. But the most significant reason for anticipating a shortage of teachers is the rising birthrate at a time when the number of students preparing themselves for teaching is falling sharply.

With the declining birthrate all through the Sixties, the number of babies born in the United States reached a low point of 3.1 million each year in the early Seventies, but since then has risen steadily to 3.6 million in 1982. These babies will be in elementary school before 1990, in high school in the late 1990s, and ready for college in the year 2000. Unless the number of teacher candidates rises sharply, there will not be nearly enough teachers to staff our schools and colleges.

The U.S. Department of Education estimates that between the years 1985 and 2000 the school-age population will increase by 17.6% but will be very unevenly distributed across the country. While it is expected to *decline* by 12% in the mid-Atlantic states and remain unchanged in the Great Lakes states, it is projected to increase by 60% in the Rocky Mountain states, by 46% in the Southwestern states, and by 35% in the Far West.[3] If I were a student seeking a career in teaching in the years just ahead, I would try to find a position in one of these Western states and, to make certification easier, would attend a college in one of these states.

* * *

I hope that awareness of the problems discussed in this book will not discourage talented young men and women from entering our profession. Some problems will be solved; the others can be lived with. All professions have their problems. If I were making a career choice in the twenty-first century, I would have no hesitation about becoming a teacher because I firmly believe that teaching, done well, is still the most personally satisfying of all the professions as well as the one offering the greatest long-range service to the human race.

For some, the opportunities will improve. Over the past half-century the emphasis has been on keeping children in school longer with the result that many of those in high school would prefer not to be there. This created a need for teachers who could work with slow and reluctant learners.

But now that the emphasis is shifting to educational quality, there will be greater need for intellectually vigorous teachers who are liberally educated in the best sense — teachers who have a firm grasp of the world of ideas, including an understanding of the nature of the learning process and of the school's proper role in society. We shall need teachers who can discriminate between the significant and the trivial and who are sufficiently tough-minded to stand up against the anti-intellectual forces in our culture. Teachers who have these traits will be in great demand.

Postscript: April 27, 1983

Yesterday afternoon, as I was reading final proof on this book, the newspapers arrived with flaming headlines: REPORT FLUNKS AMERICAN

121

EDUCATION ... SCHOOLS RATE 'M' FOR MEDIOCRE ....
AMERICAN SCHOOLS A DISASTER AREA. The National Commission
on Excellence in Education, appointed by Secretary of Education T. H. Bell,
had just released its "Open Letter to the American People" in which it pro-
claimed: "The educational foundations of our society are being eroded by a
rising tide of mediocrity that threatens our very future as a nation and a people. . . . Our once unchallenged preeminence in commerce, industry, science
and technological innovation is being overtaken by competitors throughout
the world. . . . The ideal of academic excellence as a primary goal of schooling
seems to be fading across the board in American Education."

The Commission attacked the "smorgasbord of high school electives,"
recited a litany of negative statistics including the drop in SAT scores, and
charged that 13% of all 17-year-olds are functionally illiterate. It cited
evidence that secondary school graduates in Japan and various European nations are better educated than American high school graduates. Indeed it appears that most of the criticism is directed toward our high schools rather than
our elementary schools and colleges.

It is much too early to predict what effect this report will have on the nation's schools but it will surely receive a great deal of attention. Last evening
the major networks put it at the top of their news stories and every newspaper
I have seen gives it first-page coverage. It will be discussed in school board
meetings, legislative committees, and all the newsmagazines. No educator
should ignore it or waive it aside lightly.

On local television programs this morning, the educators interviewed are
saying that many of the charges of inferiority made by the commission do not
apply in the state of Washington. They report that our high schools have
already begun raising standards, that the SAT scores of students in this state
have always been above the national level and have not declined in recent
years, and they point to the fact that Western Washington University has
already established a scholarship fund to attract more students who score in
the upper 10% on the SAT into the teaching profession.

On national newsprograms the response of most educators has been to ask,
"Where shall we get the money necessary for raising standards?" Secretary
Bell has said that supporting the schools is a state, not a national, responsibility. President Reagan, when he was given his copy of the report in a White
House ceremony, responded, "We'll continue to work for passage of tuition
tax credits, vouchers, educational savings accounts, voluntary school prayer,
and abolishing the Department of Education." He said nothing about providing more federal support for the schools.

Some of the highlights of the recommendations from the Commission on
Excellence are that:

1. School districts and state legislatures strongly consider a seven-hour
school day, as well as a school year of 200 or 220 days instead of the present
180.

2. All students seeking a high school diploma be required to take four years of English, three years of math, three years of science, three years of social studies, and a half-year of computer science.

3. All colleges raise their entrance standards.

4. Teachers get higher pay while using an effective system that includes peer review to weed out inferior teachers.

5. High school students be assigned much more homework.

6. Parents demand more of their children.

Most of the legislators so far interviewed applaud the report but quickly add that the amount of money spent on schools already is excessive. School administrators are saying that a longer school day and year would increase the school budget by 20%. (Increasing the school year would indeed increase the cost but some of the other recommendations would not. A shift from the smorgasboard curriculum to one that includes only the basic academic subjects might reduce costs.)

It is clearly true that standards for high school graduation have declined in many schools, largely because of the public demand that all students be kept in school until graduation regardless of their motivation, interest, intellectual capacity, or proneness to disruptive behavior. This demand makes high school teaching much more difficult than it was when slow or poorly motivated students were given failing grades and allowed to drop out. It made it necessary to recruit teachers who would work patiently with slow and reluctant learners, and to offer easier courses.

We can't have it both ways. We cannot require a stiff academic curriculum for every student and demand high levels of scholarly attainment while at the same time retaining all students until graduation. To maintain high standards we shall need teachers who will hold students to those standards even though the result will be more failures and dropouts. We shall need administrators who have the courage to defend such teachers. We shall have to make some provision, out of school, for the increased number of dropouts who are not ready for the job market.

Are the American people ready for that? I have my doubts, but perhaps the report of the Commission on Excellence will move public opinion in that direction.

---

1. "Foreword" *McGuffey's Sixth Reader* (New York: New American Library, 1963), p. xxii.

2. *Chronicle of Higher Education*, 26 January 1983, p. 11. Figures from Alexander W. Astin *The American Freshman: National Norms for Fall, 1982*, (Los Angeles: American Council of Education and Univ. of California, 1982).

3. *Education Week*, 14 April 1982, p. 14.